MW00579090

AND THE CHILDREN SHALL LEAD US

HOW A SELF-SUSTAINING BUSINESS MODEL IS TRANSFORMING RURAL AFRICAN VILLAGES THROUGH LOVE

BARRY CHILDS

WITH
PHILIP WHITELEY

BREAKTHROUGH BOOKS

First published in Great Britain in 2024 by Breakthrough Books.

Print ISBN: 9781739379377

The rights of Barry Childs and Philip Whiteley to be identified as the authors of this Work have been asserted by them in accordance with the Copyright, Designs and Patents Act 1988.

Copyright © 2024 by Barry Childs and Philip Whiteley

All rights reserved.

No part of this book may be reproduced in any form or by any electronic or mechanical means, including information storage and retrieval systems, without written permission from the author, except for the use of brief quotations in a book review.

Cover design by Kevyn Gilbert.

CONTENTS

PREFACE

In the past 30 years, extreme poverty around the world has been sharply reduced, especially in Asia and the Americas. But in the 2020s it has remained a serious problem in Africa. Around 90% of the world's households suffering extreme poverty are in sub-Saharan Africa. 50% of those households are concentrated in just five countries: the Democratic Republic of Congo, Madagascar, Tanzania, Nigeria and Ethiopia.

Poverty is neither inevitable nor acceptable. Africa's people are as brilliant as any in the world – the causes of poverty have been that the continent's unparalleled natural riches have attracted conquest and exploitation for centuries, while weak governance has hampered recovery. There are opportunities now to put an end to the vicious cycle of low investment, thwarted ambitions and emigration.

The Africa Bridge model is a way of transforming communities by switching from subsistence agriculture to a thriving, sustainable approach without the need for large capital investment. It retains employment and engagement of the community, instead of replacing smallholdings with large farms run by an elite.

Since its launch in 2000, the Africa Bridge model in Tanzania has lifted more than 10,000 children out of extreme poverty, and created economic benefits and new economic prospects for more than 70,000 people through projects in 37 villages. It focuses on the whole community, not just technology or the world of work, using the concept of the 'Most Vulnerable Children', and placing as a core strategic aim that no child should go hungry or lack opportunity for a fulfilling life. Local people take the lead in the projects, including children themselves, whose voices are listened to.

We have found that the focus on the welfare and prospects of the children has had multiple benefits, direct and indirect. It doesn't only improve health, housing and education for the children directly helped, it gives hope to the whole community. It is an investment in the community's future – helping society, the economy and families simultaneously. It means there is a focus on a cause around which the whole community can unite and agree. Additionally, the focus on those too young to own assets helps ensure that the initiatives are less political and more straightfor-wardly humanitarian.

I founded the Africa Bridge project with a small team of colleagues in 2000. It has demonstrated proof of concept, with strong social and economic returns. For example, the proportion of families eating three meals a day has risen from 11% to 96% after four years as part of the co-operative, and the proportion of children with a mattress or bed from 13% to 87%. Children go from eating protein a few times a month to several times a week; for the first time in their lives many children regularly attend school and partici-pate in a health plan. The local leadership of Africa Bridge, the system of reinvesting profits and sharing rewards, provides a high degree of organizational resilience. It involves intensive training and transfer of leadership to those directly involved, giving them emotional ownership of the agricultural projects.

The model holds the promise, through intensive education and training to encourage wider uptake of the approach, to make a decisive contribution to reducing extreme poverty and transforming prospects for a wider population within sub-Saharan Africa.

For hundreds of years, agricultural policies have been based on an assumption that the choice lies between an inefficient system of dispersed smallholdings, held by farmers primarily serving their family and a local market; and large farms that replace such small-holdings, in some cases dedicated to a single crop. Much human displacement, and even bloodshed, has resulted from the conflict between these two systems. Only in recent decades has it become apparent that these two unsatisfactory alternatives are not the only ones that are possible.

This book describes a proven alternative, based on a radically different approach. Independent analysis, both qualitative and quantitative, by leading social science academics, demonstrates the lasting effectiveness of this approach. Done properly, it is a game-changer, lifting entire communities substantially and irreversibly out of extreme poverty so that families and individuals can fulfil their potential.

Barry Childs, October 2023

FOREWORD

PROFESSOR CARL LARSON

It was the height of the AIDS pandemic, and I was sitting on a rock at the edge of a small village in Africa. I was watching a nurse taking large worms out of a small girl. It remains the most vivid memory of my life. There was a line of small children waiting for their turns with the nurse. The children called her 'Mama Liz'. She had taken her vacation, and the money she had saved to buy medical supplies, and made her yearly trip to the villages. She had a 'way' with the children and brought smiles and laughter along with her medical miracles.

Our team leader had spent an earlier evening in this village, during a rainstorm, and had watched many children waiting out the rainstorm huddled under trees. The AIDS pandemic had killed so many parents that the remaining children literally overwhelmed the capacities of villages to care for them.

The research we were doing led me to the work of Barry Childs, and his organization, Africa Bridge. This book tells Barry's and Africa Bridge's story. He has brought to this enterprise his knowledge and experience from a career in senior management of a highly regarded health care products corporation, the funds to provide resources which bring greater health and vitality to villages, and most importantly, a certain kind of energy.

It is not philanthropy: the agricultural, co-operative entities set up through Africa Bridge are sustainable businesses. Direct help from a charitable organization is phased out over a five-year period, following which the established enterprises help encourage wider economic development in the communities.

Those of us who have researched and evaluated a great variety of programs call this energy, and this type of engaged leadership, 'integrative'. It brings people together. It creates a process that builds confidence and promotes collective effort. It leads to experimentation and creativity. And most importantly, it brings a sense of having contributed to a better world.

Child's work is on the front edge of what is now becoming preferred strategies for dealing with poverty in Sub-Saharan Africa. The United Nations and organizations which publish recommendations for charitable giving stress the importance of women playing a central role in starting and sustaining programmatic assistance, as well as involving children in imagining and creating important aspects of village life. We see this in Africa Bridge.

Read this book and stay in touch with its message: ordinary people can do extraordinary things. We are all capable of living fuller and 'better' lives.

Dr Carl Larson, Professor Emeritus and past Dean of Social Sciences, University of Denver

PART ONE
WHAT AFRICA BRIDGE DOES

CHAPTER 1
WHAT AFRICA BRIDGE HAS DONE FOR PEOPLE

"The Africa Bridge (AB) model has the capacity to transform the lives of Tanzania's most vulnerable and impoverished children and significantly alleviate extreme poverty."

I was born in Africa. When I was a child, I played with the local children in Tanzanian villages. Yet my prospects were very different. I had all the basics every child is entitled to, and opportunities to pursue my dreams. What is the difference between these children and me? I am no brighter or more talented. It is just random luck. Instead of being born to parents living in extreme poverty, I was born to parents living in comparative abundance.

The aim of Africa Bridge is to transform the lives and prospects of children in rural communities affected by poverty. Increasingly, we can demonstrate proof of the concept. The quote at the beginning of this chapter is from a report summarizing an academic study into a five-year Africa Bridge project published in 2021. The research project was headed by Dr Heath Prince of the University of Texas, and carried out by specialists in social and economic development at the agency MarketShare Associates. The findings are discussed more fully in Chapter 3 How Africa Bridge Operates.

But before the data, the stories. The word 'transform' is strong –
and it is now a research finding, not a claim or an ambition. The
following cases are some examples of what it means.

Bariki's boys

In November 2002, the earliest days of Africa Bridge, I was
visiting my friend and mentor, Dr Mark Jacobson, founder of the
Selian Lutheran Hospital in Arusha, Tanzania. Paulina, the hospice
nurse, took me on her rounds. It was a humbling experience.

At the beginning of this millennium, few Tanzanians had access
to antiretroviral drugs. There was no well-funded national safety net
such as the social security programs in many wealthier countries.
Villagers were living on about $1 to $2 per day; people who were
sick had even less.

We visited a woman who had many symptoms of HIV/AIDS.
We talked, said prayers and sang. Then we went to see Bariki, a man
with late-stage AIDS. He was hours away from death. An old
woman sat in the shade of a tree nearby. Bariki had two children
aged seven and four. His wife had already died from AIDS, so both
boys were looking after their father. Paulina and I helped to bathe
Bariki. The woman under the tree was Grandma. She was too frail
to move. After Bariki died, she would become the children's
guardian. What was the future for these boys?

I never discovered what happened to them, but this encounter
was one of the incidents that triggered the establishment of Africa
Bridge. By listening, building on strengths and being present in, and
aware of, village realities, Africa Bridge has found a way to transform the lives of children like Bariki's boys.

Tunsi

At a team meeting with our Tanzanian staff in Tukuyu in 2014, we were discussing some of the success stories of our co-op members. Willick, our accountant, told me: 'Papa Barry, in Masoko Ward there is a woman co-op member who has become a banana trader. She is very successful.' We were going to visit the villages of Masoko the next day, so I asked Willick to get in touch with her and arrange a meeting.

Towards the end of our meeting in Lufumbi, one of the villages in Masoko Ward, a woman in a fine Kanga joined us. I wondered if this was the woman about whom Willick was speaking and, sure enough, at the end of the meeting he introduced her to me as the successful banana trader. She smiled at me and I looked into her eyes. She was someone I recognized, yet I could scarcely believe the transformation.

I had first met Tunsi Belega six years before. She had just been selected to be a founder member of the Lufumbi Village Corn Co-operative. She was destitute. Her husband had died earlier in the year, leaving her to care for three young children. She was living in a small one-room mud hut. Her face was drawn. She looked defeated. Later I questioned the wisdom of selecting her as a founder member of a co-op. She was so vulnerable. There were challenges with the first corn crop, the rainfall in 2009 was poor. However, Tunsi and the other 11 members of the co-op persisted. The abundant rains in 2011 made for an excellent crop. Her family began to flourish; the children went to school, they ate three meals a day, they built a bigger house and could afford luxuries such as oil and lamplight in the evenings.

Tunsi told me that after the monthly corn co-op meetings, the women would continue their discussions on their own. They began to realize that they were growing better quality corn than the men. Tunsi said, 'If we can grow corn better than the men, then we can do anything better than the men.'

Tunsi then started a banana trading business. She rented large trucks to transport plantains to the markets in Mbeya 50 miles away.

Then she widened her scope to Iringa, 200 miles away, and then Dar es Salaam, 550 miles away. This is phenomenal. Trading of this nature has always been a man's world. She had much to negotiate – truck rentals, drivers, loaders, overnight security and dealing with buyers. This seemingly frail woman from a small village was breaking the mold.

She built a modern house in the nearby town of Tukuyu, near a good secondary school and all the amenities of the town. By the time of beginning to write this book in 2020-2021, during the Covid pandemic, Tunsi had turned to farming ginger, which is used extensively in Tanzania as a prophylactic against the virus.

All her children are doing well. Her eldest daughter has graduated from college as a teacher and her other children go to a good secondary school. Tunsi said, 'What I enjoy most in my spare time is to sit with other women and discuss how we can be successful in business.'

Jacob

By 2007 Jacob, a resident of a village that later hosted an Africa Bridge project, had seen his four adult children die of HIV/AIDS, leaving him and his wife Garannetti to care for their eight grandchildren. On an income of approximately $400 per year he had no hope of giving his family a good life. In 2008 Jacob was nominated by his village Most Vulnerable Children's Committee to become a founder member of the Bujesi Cow Co-op. After three months' training he received a nine-month-old heifer which he named Tumaini, meaning hope.

Tumaini has transformed their lives by producing seven calves, thousands of gallons of milk and mountains of dung to enrich their crops. His grandchildren now have a healthy diet, receive health care and a good education. Furthermore, the three eldest children have graduated from university, transforming both their individual prospects and those of their grandparents and wider family. The younger three grandchildren are attending university. This is a miracle in a country where only a few can even dream of university.

Granny Mary

Mary Kipesili is a grandmother who was living on less than $2 per day. She cares for her three orphaned grandchildren in the Masoko Ward located in southwestern Tanzania. Masoko is a collection of seven villages set in the beautiful foothills surrounding Mount Rungwe, the third highest mountain in Tanzania, and hosted an Africa Bridge project in the period 2008-2013. The village's Most Vulnerable Children's Committee nominated Granny Mary to become one of the 10 founder members of the newly formed village cow co-op.

She attended all the classes, such as how to run a co-op, growing and managing a pasture, building a cow shelter, managing the milk lactations, and how to feed and clean her cow. Noel Mushua, the Africa Bridge Livestock and Agriculture coordinator, together with the local government agriculture officers, were her teachers. Noel informed me that Granny Mary cannot speak Swahili, the common language in Tanzania, but only speaks Mwykusa, which is her tribal language. Nor can she read or write. So her eldest grandson, who was a student at the local secondary school, accompanied her during all the training sessions. Her grandson took notes so the family would have documentation on exactly what she needed to do to become an excellent cow keeper. Mary listened diligently and asked numerous questions.

The results are transformational. Mary's cow Job produces 14 liters of milk per day. A typical village cow will only yield 1 to 2 liters per day. Job has delivered numerous calves. Mary donated the first calf to her co-op, giving another family the opportunity to join. The second calf she reared for six months and sold. This enabled her to send her eldest grandson to a highly rated school in Arusha. The third calf she donated to her local village's Most Vulnerable Children's Committee to enable them to support vulnerable families not yet in a co-op. The fourth calf she kept to increase her milk production. The proceeds from the sale of milk have helped her to improve the family's diet, to purchase a healthcare plan and improve her house. In addition, she has also started a small business of rearing and selling chickens.

All the founder members of the Lipa Mbele (Pay it Forward) co-op donated their first-born calves to other families caring for most vulnerable children. Those new members did the same and within six years the co-op grew from 10 to 27 members.

While villagers have an innate understanding of agriculture, they do not have the support, knowledge, or the capital to acquire and manage a high-grade dairy cow. Granny Mary demonstrates that when given the relevant information, a support system and a valuable asset, vulnerable village families have the capacity to raise themselves out of extreme poverty, transforming the lives of their most vulnerable children.

Orida and Gilbert (interviewed in 2018): New uniforms today, a brighter future tomorrow

Most of us, when we walk into a dark room, can just flip a switch and there is light. If you live in a village in rural Tanzania earning $1 to $2 a day, there is no switch, and very few people even have electricity, or can afford kerosene for a lamp.

As our children grow up, we assume they will go to school. In the villages we serve this is not always so. School tuition is free, but to attend a child must have a school uniform, notebooks and a pair of shoes. Most of the families caring for vulnerable children cannot afford such supplies.

So when a pickup truck loaded with boxes of new uniforms – crisp white shirts, apple-red sweaters and navy-blue skirts for girls and shorts for boys – arrived at Kalalo Village Primary School in south-western Tanzania, Orida Mwakaja and Gilbert Agray celebrated along with their classmates, with huge smiles on their faces.

The uniforms and other school supplies were a gift to the school's Most Vulnerable Children made possible by donors to Africa Bridge.

Orida and Gilbert are proud –not just of their new uniforms, but of the education they are receiving. To realize their dreams, they study hard. Twelve-year-old Orida is in Standard 7, her last year of primary school. Although she is an orphan, Orida has big plans for her future. After completing primary school, she wants to attend secondary school for six years. Her hope is to continue her education at a university and become both a doctor and a businesswoman.

'My favorite subject is math because it will help me to make a lot of money as a businesswoman,' Orida explains. When not studying or helping with home and farm chores, Orida enjoys running.

Eleven-year-old Gilbert is in Standard 6. His favorite subject is Swahili, Tanzania's national language. Gilbert loves playing soccer and one day hopes to become an airline pilot.

Despite the new uniforms, Orida knows her school lacks some basic necessities. She says: 'My primary school's seven classrooms need more desks, glass in the window frames to keep out the cold in the winter, a toilet and — most importantly — more teachers.' Eight teachers are responsible for 427 students, with class sizes ranging from 53 to 80. Orida hopes her village will improve its schools because she believes education is important in bettering the lives of villagers.

Gilbert and Orida are proud of Kalalo Village's increased emphasis on agriculture. The village grows maize, bananas, avocados, coffee and tea, in addition to raising cows.

'I want Kalalo to be known for its agriculture,' Gilbert says.

In a country that has seen its adult population significantly reduced by the spread of HIV/AIDS, resulting in large numbers of orphans and fewer resources, children such as Orida and Gilbert understand they must overcome many challenges if they are to succeed in school and obtain the education they desire. But they also see the positive changes already happening in their own village. The cow and avocado co-operatives started by Africa Bridge empower villagers to create economically sustainable businesses, grow more food and improve schools, so that even vulnerable children and families will thrive.

Donations for new uniforms help children like Orida and Gilbert attend school today, and to start income generating co-operatives to ensure they can go to school tomorrow.

Lwitiko

When Africa Bridge starts work in any community, we begin by listening to the children. As we began our intervention in the village of Igembe in 2008, we sat on makeshift benches together with the villagers under a beautiful shade tree. After the introductory protocol, the village Chairman introduced us to one of the many orphans. His name was Lwitiko. The Chairman then did something most unusual. He asked Lwitiko to present the formal village profile. Typically, this would be done by a village leader or an elder, not a child.

Lwitiko was a small, very thin 15-year-old boy who had just completed his Primary School education. He stood up and with great authority made the presentation. It was brilliant. It was well thought out, covering the essentials, yet short enough to maintain our attention.

Lwitiko, being an orphan, was fortunate to have received any education. However, his prospects of going to a good high school and perhaps gaining a college diploma seemed non-existent. Lwitiko excelled in school and the villagers considered him a genius, but at the time he could not conceive of ever leaving the village. Given the circumstances there was no way to further his education.

Soon after this meeting Africa Bridge established a Most Vulnerable Children's Committee and started two in Igembe. While these initiatives were helping to lift the economic recovery of the villages, Lwitiko benefited from some direct support for his education from his aunt, a donor and myself, and some further facilitation from myself and a staff member at Africa Bridge, on the basis of his exceptional potential. Six years later in the spring of 2014, he graduated from a high school for gifted children with distinctions in every subject. In October 2014 he started medical school. In July 2018 I received an e-mail from Lwitiko describing what he had learned during a three-month placement at Durham University Medical School in Great Britain.

In November 2019 Lwitiko graduated as a doctor, second in his class of 165 students. His dream is to return to Igembe to practise medicine and start a community health initiative using the principles he has learned from Africa Bridge.

Lwitiko started life as a normal village child. At the age of nine he was orphaned, and his life fell into chaos with no hope of escaping a grim fate. Today he is living his dream.

This is what Africa Bridge is all about.

SUMMARY

At his inaugural address in 1992, Nelson Mandela said that we are all brilliant, gorgeous, talented and fabulous. We are all born to manifest the glory of God that is in each one of us. As we shine our light on others, we liberate them to share their talents and gifts.

The donors, supporters, volunteers, staff, board members and founder of Africa Bridge want to shine our light on the millions of children like Lwitiko and allow them to be Brilliant, Gorgeous, Talented and Fabulous. The stories in this chapter have been replicated hundreds of times in the more than 20 years that the Africa Bridge co-operative movement has been operational.

They also indicate that there is still much to learn about the most effective approaches that development programs need to take, which may mean altering or abandoning more conventional tactics and strategies. In the next chapter, we describe the philosophy and basic concepts of the Africa Bridge approach, and how it differs from other economic and development programs.

CHAPTER 2
DIFFERENT WAYS OF THINKING

C hildren are the future of any family or community, and a focus on improving their prospects can also help communities in the present. This is the focus that makes Africa Bridge different. It is radically different both from aid programs, and from conventional agricultural policies. Instead of treating the matter as a question of land reform, or redistribution, or a return on assets in the case of economic development, the focus is on the people; specifically, how to improve the lives and prospects of the most vulnerable children.

Maintaining a focus at all times on the wellbeing of children is the way we approach programs. This chapter describes the key differences in policy and approach, while details of how the agricultural co-operatives and the Most Vulnerable Children Committees work will be described in Chapter 3 How Africa Bridge Operates. We have constructed a policy and a methodology that works backwards from human needs, rather than starting with plans for infrastructure and territory and expecting the people to work around them.

Success is measured by the sustainability of the project and improved outcomes for the most vulnerable children. While success is not defined solely by financial returns on physical assets like a conventional business investment, the projects do aim to set up viable businesses that are regenerative and self-sustaining.

There has been a significant amount of research into the difference between successful and unsuccessful agricultural projects in developing regions since the 1990s, and some findings are starting to emerge. These informed the setting up of Africa Bridge in the early 2000s, while our own experience has provided an exercise in action learning, in turn adding to the research base which will hopefully benefit others involved in social and economic development.

Dr Carl Larson, Emeritus Professor of Human Communication at Denver University and an academic adviser to Africa Bridge, has several decades worth of relevant experience in effective social change programs. The findings indicate that the key to success is the degree of integration and involvement of the whole community. He says:

'If you look at the last couple of decades, issues have been raised with regards to the impact of microfinancing. Some of the answers lie in process quality. Analyses have suggested mixed results, and that sometimes interventions have caused more harm than good. The UN in the 2010s sought to establish a set of principles based on findings, guided by health and social progress. The principles that emerge all reinforce the importance of being integrative and collaborative, involving women. This brings into question the approach of being redistributive. When you don't focus on being collective but are redistributive – this can cause problems. This is reinforced by Harvard's index of social progress. Both show similar results: an emphasis on redistribution with inequity caused more harm, even in the poorest areas.'

He adds: 'In agricultural villages if you are not careful you can disrupt integrative processes and change to one that is not reliant on collaboration and building identity. With Africa Bridge, 20 years ago it recognized these problems and adopted integrative processes. This involves empowering women and building collective identity, and collaborative problem-solving. This approach is where the rest of the world in development and aid is heading. In assessment, we make sure the factors that we measure are those seen by people in their contexts. We [at Denver University] have done this for many different organizations.'

The integrative approach to leadership is also discussed in Chapter 8 Women take a Leading Role, while the importance of purpose and passion is discussed in the Chapter 10 Love is a Verb.

With the focus on the community and seeking to boost the health and prospects of the most vulnerable children, we have aimed to avoid the pitfalls of two more established approaches to development, namely traditional aid programs and microfinancing through a bank.

Traditional aid programs

These involve direct assistance to communities affected by poverty. They can have long-term benefits, for example when funding education and health programs. But they can also result in dependence. If there is no viable cluster of businesses established, the community becomes vulnerable to aid programs being cut owing to financial stress affecting donors, often in a very different economy, or to changes of priority in those deciding on aid budgets.

Microfinance through a bank

This can help start-ups in deprived communities. The advantage over aid programs is that, if businesses become profitable they are self-sustaining and do not require aid or subsidies; moreover, they can stimulate entrepreneurial and technical expertise, helping to create a cluster of businesses and thus drive economic development. But the downside is that the banks will need a financial return within a certain timeframe, causing uncertainty and economic fragility if businesses struggle to move into profit. The focus of the banks is on the assets and returns, not on the community.

At Africa Bridge, we do look for returns – but in a multi-dimensional way: in the community, through social, health and educational benefits, but economically also. We have a track record of seeking to encourage entrepreneurialism and business clusters, which generate wealth locally to the benefit of the community. There is a focus on empowering entrepreneurialism, rather than aid, but with a focus on the community to avoid too much emphasis on personal enrichment. Nonetheless, the sharing of profits from the co-operatives is limited to loan repayments, savings and helping the most vulnerable children; there is greater freedom to retain profits than in the type of co-op where all profits are shared. This retention of individual entrepreneurialism helps encourage growth, innovation and reinvestment. In practice, while profit maximization is not the primary aim, some of the entrepreneurs have been highly successful, in some cases becoming serial entrepreneurs and helping create a cluster of successful enterprises, not necessarily confined to agriculture, as their skills, confidence and contacts have been strengthened. This has improved their own families' prospects and created employment opportunities for others in the community. This also opens up the possibility of assets and opportunities being passed down to the succeeding generation.

One challenge when establishing agricultural co-operatives in areas affected by poverty is that they can unintentionally cause inequity, tension and resentment between insiders and those left out. The approach of Africa Bridge seeks to minimize this hazard in two ways: firstly, by encouraging growth through new members, rather than keeping the project to a clique; and secondly, by seeking to help the whole community through the Most Vulnerable Children's Committee. If, say, you are a single parent struggling to ensure your children get to school, and do not have the aptitude or opportunity to join the co-operative, it is possible that the co-op will nevertheless provide the funds for your children's educational equipment. In this way, the constituency that is supportive of the project is as broad and strong as possible.

In addition to questions of equity is the question of how to create transparency in regard to why some people are invited to participate in the co-ops while others are not. Failure to provide convincing reasons can cause resentment. In the Africa Bridge approach, the focus on the most vulnerable, based on an in-depth initial assessment, provides a rationale for key decisions on membership. After a Most Vulnerable Children's Committee is formed, members conduct a transit walk, somewhat like a census, identifying each household in the village and their needs, as will be described more fully in Chapter 3 How Africa Bridge Operates.

Is it effective? The only way to be sure is to measure – and we have learned that multiple different types of data are necessary. This book both chronicles the findings we have recorded in the several projects across the more than 37 villages we have helped since the early 2000s and describes the more ambitious and rigorous program of research we are launching with this publication – with the hope of disseminating the Africa Bridge concept across different regions of Africa, and perhaps even beyond.

We seek to engage the whole community. Women assume leadership roles – it is a founding requirement that at least 50% of the members of a Most Vulnerable Childrens' Committee and an agricultural co-operative are women. In practice, the proportion of members who are women is typically higher, around two-thirds. In some villages, some of the adult male population has migrated to a city to find work, from where they remit money home, so meeting the 50% requirement has not been difficult.

We have found that women tend to be more vested in nurturing and protecting children and in building communities, so empowering them helps the whole society, and helps ensure sustainability for the projects. Our focus is on building upon strengths, rather than simply solving problems.

•   •   •

Measure by program, rather than nation or region

With any social program, how do you know if the investments and initiatives are effective?

Traditional economic statistics and social indicators that are aggregated across a region may give a helpful general overview. But they lack detail when it comes to assessing effectiveness. There is growing recognition in the field of economic development that more useful insights are derived by assessing impact by program, rather than by region. There are two perceived advantages here: a clearer focus on whether conditions are actually improving, and a greater ability to gauge cause-and-effect relationships. Limiting one's focus to a particular program, one can engage in quantitative and qualitative studies linking particular investments and actions to the effects on individuals, society or the environment.

Greater impetus for this shift comes from research findings showing that initiatives to help regions affected by poverty, such as microfinance for business start-ups and agricultural co-operatives, vary considerably in their effectiveness. As noted, some may cause local inequalities and a perception of unfairness. Failure rates of agricultural co-operatives in certain conditions can be quite high.

Since Africa Bridge was founded in 2000, with the first co-ops established in 2005, we have sought to gauge the impact and to be pragmatic: dropping practices that fail and encouraging those that are more effective, with success measured by quality-of-life indicators for the most vulnerable children and their families.

Over the years, we have sought to introduce more rigor. For example, to begin with we asked the teachers for a list of the most vulnerable children in the community; then we moved towards carrying out a more thorough census, following establishment of the Most Vulnerable Children's Committees (MVCCs). With each program, we take a baseline at the start and at the end. This initially consisted of quantitative data (such as number of meals with protein per day, whether attending school or sleeping in a bed). From 2021 we have included more qualitative findings and have sought to collaborate with independent research specialists. Qualitative insights are based on questionnaires asking participants about prospects, effectiveness of interventions, and quality of life.

Our findings confirm the observation Dr Carl Larson makes: that integrative approaches, involving the whole community, are more likely to lead to sustained effectiveness. In 2008 in the Masoko Ward, with the support of the Rotary Club in Portland, Oregon, we began to ensure that, in our programs, the MVCCs and the agricultural co-operatives worked closely together. A levy on agricultural profits funded the MVCC, and there was some shared membership of the two groups. There is more detailed discussion on how the two entities work together in the next chapter.

MVCCs had been started by the Tanzanian Government, but they were not always sustainable on their own, sometimes lacking adequate training and resources. A successful co-operative helped rectify these deficiencies and, in practice, the two became natural partners.

In late 2019 I visited all the wards and asked participants what had worked, what had failed.

In the 2020s, we are deepening and formalizing research into our effectiveness, in partnership with leading academics from the University of Texas. The approach is based around a Theory of Change, which is applicable when limited to study of a particular program. This will be discussed in greater depth in Chapter 5 Theory of Change and Emerging Principles.

Limits of traditional economic indicators

Conventional economic indicators such as gross domestic product (GDP) have long been recognized as superficial and inadequate for monitoring social progress. For example, a grandiose infrastructure project, not geared to the needs of the local community, boosts GDP but may do little to alleviate poverty. The indicator of GDP-per-capita provides a weighting for population, but it is an average, so does not reflect inequality, nor does it give information on economic opportunities, quality of employment opportunities or quality of living conditions.

The Ray Marshall Center at the University of Texas, Austin, a research partner to Africa Bridge, has developed more sophisticated indicators that include measures of individual and household well-being. They have worked with the non-governmental organization Nuru International to gather relevant data and develop this multi-dimensional approach – including, for example, diet and health – working at program level outcomes, rather than at national level. This has led to the development of indices used to measure household and community resilience resulting from Nuru's interventions. The Center also uses an approach known as the Multidimensional Poverty Index (MPI), developed by Oxford University. It is based on an assessment of a range of critical defined deprivations at the household level, such as education, health outcomes, ownership of assets and access to services. Such an approach offers a much fuller and more useful portrait of acute poverty than simple income measures and, if monitored over time, enables a detailed measure of which interventions are effective.

Dr Heath Prince, director and research scientist at the Ray Marshall Center, says: 'We have gotten smart over what works in terms of sustainable co-operatives, engaging communities. We have developed indices that measure not just the outcomes of interventions but resilience of communities over time.'

The international standard measure for extreme poverty is having to survive on less than $1.90 a day. While all would agree that this is too low, significant increases might have a varying impact on quality of life, depending on numerous other factors that one can only assess at the level of the community or family. In addition, as Heath indicates, it helps to have an indication as to how durable or sustainable any improvements may be. For such insights, it is necessary to investigate more thoroughly.

∙   ∙   ∙

The Research Program: How effective is Africa Bridge?

Gauging the impact of an intervention, rather than measuring aggregate economic or social indicators across a region, helps both researchers and program directors understand more clearly any causal links between policies and outcomes. It helps to have a blend of quantitative and qualitative surveys in order to enrich the quality of intelligence. This is increasingly well understood and accepted in the social sciences, according to our academic advisers.

Quantitative findings indicate what is happening; qualitative surveys yield insights into why. In the context of Africa Bridge, quantitative indicators might include the increased numbers of children having protein in their meals every day and the proportion attending school. Qualitative, questionnaire-based surveys can indicate *why*: whether increased income for a household is through better yields, or more educated individuals gaining a salaried post through better access to education, or a combination. Perhaps an agricultural initiative failed, but with the skills gained co-operative members had the ability and confidence to set up other entrepreneurial activities. Attendance at school might be affected by local transport, higher income to pay for uniforms and equipment, or whether children are relieved of domestic caring responsibilities. Surveys may also include questions about perceptions of quality of life.

In turn, this informs the *how*: which specific strategies, tactics, and skills are statistically more likely to reduce poverty and improve living conditions. Analysis of qualitative information across a population helps identify which parts of an initiative are most effective, both in achieving the quantitatively assessed outcomes, and the more subjective responses around quality of life.

For Africa Bridge, we are ambitious. Our ambition is not to grow large in organizational size, but rather through influence. Africa Bridge is definitely *not* trademark protected or patented! We welcome imitations. Indeed, the closer to our approach, the better, unless others can identify improvements, in which case we would welcome feedback to inform our own approach. The wider ambition is for this approach to make a sizeable impact in terms of reducing poverty and increasing life prospects. We are confident we have achieved this for around 10,000 most vulnerable children and about 20,000 other family members. The exciting part comes if and when we extend this to millions, by encouraging take-up of the model.

For the approach to be copied, using what one could loosely term a franchise model, there has to be a methodology that is both copiable and proven. Hence for this period of development of Africa Bridge, there is a considerable emphasis upon research by independent academics. It can go against the humanitarian instinct to set aside money for these investments, rather than put everything directly into programs, but of course the savings from understanding which are the most effective approaches mean that the investment can be recouped many times over, and many more people can be reached.

Starting in 2021, Africa Bridge has embarked on a three-phase research project, in partnership with academic institutions and specialist research consultancies:

Phase I

Africa Bridge has commitments from researchers at University of Texas, University of Denver and MarketShare Associates to evaluate the quantitative and qualitative impacts of the program in Kisondela in Tanzania, and other graduated wards. The researchers focus on the wellbeing of children, alleviation of extreme poverty and sustainability of the program. The Kisondela project was an Africa Bridge five-year program that completed in March 2021 (see findings in Chapter 5 Theory of Change and Emerging Principles).

Phase II

This phase is designed to demonstrate the scalability of the

Africa Bridge program by implementing its model in three new areas of Tanzania, and a region in a neighboring country. Four wards consisting of around 20 villages, potentially impacting 50,000 residents, and 8,000 vulnerable children will be identified as likely subjects for this research, with some decisions depending on the outcome of Phase 1. The impacts will then be compared with a control group of wards not involved in the program.

Phase III

This phase involves making the model available to other non-governmental organizations (NGOs), charitable foundations, and governments to implement in countries other than Tanzania. In this phase, Africa Bridge will implement a communications and outreach plan to share the concept with international media, governments, and other institutions, including the international health care community. We will work in either a partnership arrangement or an open-source arrangement. Africa Bridge will continue to operate in Tanzania and continue to improve the model and explore other applications.

SUMMARY

Africa Bridge has been set up and run on distinctive principles. These were based on the author's experience, both as a child, the son of a specialist agricultural adviser, and as a multifunctional executive trained in the quality movement and effective team-work. In turn, they have been refined through learning-by-doing in the early years of the project, which has been running for more than 20 years. We feel that there are enough empirical findings to justify continuing with and expanding the programs, especially given the transformation of life prospects that we have seen. The next steps are to deepen and formalize such learnings and to disseminate them to others with similar ambitions. How a program actually operates in practice is the subject of the next chapter.

KEY POINTS

- The Africa Bridge approach starts with the perspective of the most vulnerable children in a community and works back to develop programs that will help improve their prospects.
- There is an emphasis on creating sustainable and regenerative projects.
- It differs from traditional aid programs by creating businesses, and from conventional business investment by measuring returns both in social and financial terms – with entrepreneurialism and social development encouraged.
- In the field of economic development, there is increasing emphasis upon measuring by program, rather than by nation or region, so as to understand better cause-and-effect relationships between investments and social outcomes.
- A combination of quantitative and qualitative measures are necessary to understand the impact of social programs. The former indicates what is happening, and the latter gives intelligence as to why.
- The Africa Bridge organization is investing in in-depth, independent academic analysis, with a view both to demonstrating its effectiveness to others considering such an approach, and to indicating which strategies work best. The ambition is that this learning will encourage widespread imitation of the approach, potentially lifting millions out of extreme poverty.

CHAPTER 3
HOW AFRICA BRIDGE OPERATES

4 August 2002

am attending a meeting at the Idweli village council, western Tanzania. It follows months of planning. We are finalizing arrangements for a 'Future Search' meeting – a conference to prepare the way for an Africa Bridge project to begin – due to take place on 8, 9 and 10 November. The village office is a small mud brick building with a tin roof and small windows that do not open. There is a broken desk, a table, a few chairs and hard benches on which to sit. Mr Ngeka the village Chairman, together with the village secretary, the head teacher, Furaha my interpreter from the NGO Godfrey's Children Organization and I sit at the table, facing the men sitting on benches and the women sitting on the floor at the back of the room.

It is a clear day, the sun bakes the tin roof. The air is stuffy and the participants equally stuffy. The protocol and formality of the men is stifling the free flow of information. Some progress is being made; however, I have much riding on the success of this meeting and I am becoming bored and frustrated by the self-important behavior being demonstrated by the men. I reflect that if we are going to make any impact on the community we have to hear everyone's voices.

Suddenly, injecting a different and more lively tone than the speeches of the men, we hear an excited group of children laughing and playing as they run past the building. Their infectious glee lifts the mood a little and acts as a spur to my thinking. The whole purpose of Africa Bridge – the founding vision – is to transform prospects for the most vulnerable children, yet I suddenly realize they are on the wrong side of the wall.

I feel that something is missing. I get up and request that I be excused for a 'chimba dawa', literally translated as a dig for herbs, but understood as a request for a comfort break. As I walk out into the nearby woods, blinking a little at the sudden change from gloom to sunlight, the thought I had in the room begins to be fleshed out in my mind as an idea. The children are the clients, they are the focus. Why not – heretical thought – not only involve them, but let them lead the discussion? The conversations that follow, within the community and with Africa Bridge, result in our settling upon this radical idea.

Conventionally, in social and economic development programs, the process begins with the perspective of policy makers, donors, or asset owners plus politicians. If a program is decided upon, these leaders inform local administrators and professionals and then consult with the community, but only the adults, if at all. We were going to turn this communication process upside down. We decided to start with the children's description of their context. We were not going to place leadership responsibility on their shoulders, as that would have been an unfair burden, but we wanted to start with their point of view, as they would know their context better than any administrator. We viewed the children as the ultimate clients, as the strategic purpose of Africa Bridge was to transform their prospects for the better.

Would it work?

Future Search

We incorporated this idea of listening to the children's perspective first, letting them set the context, within a more established approach, known as Future Search (https://futuresearch.net/about/whatis/). Core elements of Future Search are not new, and not unique to Africa Bridge – they have been practised in many commercial and non-profit organizations for years. In early 2002 Margaret Wheatley, author of multiple books on leadership, introduced me to the founders of Future Search, who trained me to be a facilitator. The concept is to gather together all key actors for a discussion, typically lasting around 20 hours, spread over three days, to talk about our past, present, and desired future. It is a foundational set of meetings and forms the basis for subsequent programs and investments. The result of a well run Future Search set of meetings is a deep understanding of each other's backgrounds, realities, motivations and ambitions.

Principles of Future Search are:

- To get the 'whole system' into the same room. To this end, representatives of all key constituencies are involved, including those with authority, resources, expertise, information and need.
- To explore the whole problem, before dividing it into constituent parts; to understand the real context.
- Put the common ground, and the future focus, front and center, while treating problems and conflicts as information rather than action items.
- Encourage self-management and responsibility for actions by all participants.

In practice, we have found this to be valuable – indeed, essential – in preparing a foundation for a successful project. It means the start of a project is grounded in a deep and shared understanding of the group's context and ambitions. It also helps to identify individuals who are capable of being facilitators to deploy for the programs.

We had begun in Idweli following a request from Dr Neema Mgana, a United Nations adviser, fiancée to Godfrey Nsemwa, a charismatic doctor, since deceased, who had travelled overseas to give talks at conferences. Godfrey had been born in Idweli, and the village at the time was affected by issues of poverty, including a high rate of orphans, mostly caused by AIDS but made even worse by the tragic death of more than 40 adults as a result of a petrol tanker overturning and catching fire in 2001. It was in this year that Godfrey died, and his family created an NGO called Godfrey's Children Organization in his honor. Neema contacted me when she was studying for her Master's in Public Health in the US, and asked me to go to Idweli and do a 'Needs Analysis' to determine how to help the orphans in Idweli. Between us we decided that the best thing to do was a Future Search.

Focus on the children

Once a suitable candidate for the Africa Bridge approach is selected, we begin our discussions with the community and prepare for the initial Future Search meetings. In practice we hold two Future Searches, and the first is just with the children. They are aged 10 to 20, representing all the villages of the ward. This phase typically lasts for three days. The children elect representatives from each village, from among them, to speak at the second Future Search meeting.

The second round also lasts three days. We have a rest day in the middle, so the process in total covers a week. For each three-day session, there are four agenda items. The first is: what's the history and context of the most vulnerable children – not only in the village and in Tanzania, but in the world, and for me personally, in the case of the children themselves? We gather together multiple points of view on the issue. The second agenda item is: describe the reality of a most vulnerable child in your community today. That often produces some very sad stories. One interesting feature is that, particularly with the children, the most graphic descriptions do not come from those who are most vulnerable themselves but are related by others more fortunate. Those who are most vulnerable are often reluctant to contribute directly – perhaps because they are too close to the experiences, or perhaps because they feel a sense of shame. Others describe the experiences on their behalf, often most eloquently.

The third agenda item is: how would I want this to be? We invite the children to imagine a wizard has come and given everyone a sweet – some of them may never have had a sweet before. Then we ask them to imagine a potion that enables you to wake up in 15 years' time. We ask them to describe how they would like things to be. It doesn't have to be practical – just dream. Then the fourth agenda is: how do we get from Phase Two to Phase Three? That's when they come up with plans and ideas. It is the children who open the second three-day Future Search conference. Children from each village who are elected as representatives to present to the adults prepare for this second phase on the rest day, with support and advice from Africa Bridge staff.

On the very first occasion we ran the process in this way, those of us involved in this socially risky, unprecedented initiative were nervous. I was there with Martha Mmbando, who helped me set up Africa Bridge, and who was to join full-time from 1 January 2003, a few weeks after the inaugural Future Search at Idweli, as the first employee. In addition, we had two volunteers from the Future Search consultancy, one from the US and one from Sweden, plus the head of the Lundy Foundation. Our level of confidence that letting the children lead the discussions would be productive was, it's fair to say, below 100%. We were worrying what would happen, but we decided to trust the process. We just shut up. The children were indeed candid – and I recall thinking that perhaps we received more than we bargained for. When we asked them to describe reality, they described everything, including drinking, sexual practices among the adults, and how these activities impacted them. To begin with, the adults were indignant. Then, there were expressions of shame, with some adults openly crying. Curiously, however, after letting the dynamics run their course, there was a further shift in sentiment. Some of the parents expressed pride that their children had had the courage to stand up and say how it was and do so in an honest and articulate manner. Perhaps there was a sense of relief among some of the grown-ups that some taboo issues were finally being discussed and addressed. We had a fabulous Future Search meeting. Every time we do this, we repeat that process. We say to facilitators who haven't seen it before, who perhaps are tempted to question our sanity: No, trust the children.

Children bring transparency. Without their views, we wouldn't learn about many challenges within the villages – or, indeed, strengths. They have a greater tendency to speak with candor, without a filter, which means that we learn about strengths and weaknesses in the community much more quickly. Examples of challenges could be drinking habits by adults, or a child who is not the biological son or daughter of the head of the household being treated less favorably. A hidden strength may be a kindly neighbor who helps children. We ask both children and adults about matters that are a source of pride, or of shame. For all the difficult and sensitive issues that arise, we have never experienced interpersonal conflicts arising from the discussions becoming out of control. Much sensitivity is required by facilitators – we train them to ask questions, not offer opinions, and to encourage open and mutually respectful discussions, both among adults and children.

. . .

A village is too small

One important lesson that we learned, and it took a while to learn this, was that a village is too small to be a viable partner with an NGO, even a small one. After a couple of years working with Idweli, I realized that we needed to work with a collection of villages to have the necessary personnel and resources. An Africa Bridge project is based on a small regional unit known as a ward. A ward is a collection of villages, typically somewhere between three and seven. Selection of a suitable ward is made through a consultative process. Africa Bridge representatives begin by initiating a discussion with a local government body, a district council, informing them that we are ready to begin a new project. They will call a meeting of the district council, made up of Ward councillors representing each ward. We request that they propose to us candidate wards for a project. In practice, wards are keen to put themselves forward, owing to the track record of Africa Bridge. The district council then consults with the local communities and ask a district social work officer to produce a shortlist of wards that the council then presents to us. Based on the need and the potential, plus other considerations such as logistics and location, we select one of the wards.

Another lesson in the early years was that, while many of the agricultural projects were successful for some time, they were not always sustained, and the economic benefits did not always flow to the children. From this learning we developed the idea of the Most Vulnerable Children's Committee (MVCC), set up to work in close partnership with the co-operative, in order to combine the social and economic objectives of the enterprises.

In the current way of operation, at the end of the second Future Search session, we ask each village to elect a Ward Steering Committee member who isn't a government servant. Then each village elects and sets up an MVCC. Once this is done the MVCC can nominate, with the assistance of Africa Bridge staff, the villagers eligible to join a co-op. This listing is vetted by village and ward governments, then finalized at a meeting of the whole village.

The Africa Bridge organization funds the basic establishment of the twin entities, the training and other basic resources necessary for their foundation. The Ward Steering Committee oversees implementation. It comprises local politicians in the form of the Ward Council, plus the selected individuals from each village and relevant professionals, such as a health officer, development officer, educational professional and an administrator.

A key early recruitment decision in an Africa Bridge project is to identify and hire empowerment facilitators. This role was introduced in 2013 after identifying weaknesses in the earliest programs. These key individuals are typically younger villagers with some tertiary education, who want to remain in their communities and make a contribution rather than seek a professional career in a city. They are highly literate and numerate, and can compile reports with qualitative information and data. They are not full-time staff, but Africa Bridge pays them a stipend. They act as the first line of representatives of Africa Bridge in the village. They act as advisers and as trouble-shooters, on occasion alerting Africa Bridge managers to a problem that requires intervention, or that may require specialist agricultural or veterinarian help.

The Most Vulnerable Children's Committee, and the co-operative, are constituted as separate entities, but Africa Bridge encourages some overlap of membership between the two.

The Most Vulnerable Children's Committee (MVCC)

The MVCCs were first introduced in the Masoko Ward in 2008. Children in western Tanzania, where Africa Bridge programs have been located to date, are in some cases exceptionally deprived. Children defined as most vulnerable by Africa Bridge are those whose families, for example, cannot afford educational equipment or a uniform to attend school, or where children are eating only one meal per day with little or no protein, and may be sleeping on a mat on the ground rather than in a bed, and living in an overcrowded, poor quality house. In addition, some have been orphaned, and HIV infection rates in adults, including parents, has been an issue.

Members of the MVCC have to be literate and elected by the community; the committee must comprise at least 50% women. Much care and planning go into recruitment, training and preparation. Children are involved from the beginning and are encouraged to have their say and influence decisions.

One of the first actions of the MVCC, together with the local government social worker and Africa Bridge staff, is to carry out a 'transit walk' to establish which households care for most vulnerable children, and to ascertain their vulnerability. They visit every household and check for the most vulnerable. They draw up a list of households with the village's most vulnerable children, in approximate order of vulnerability. Criteria could include:

- Whether the child regularly attends school,
- Underlying health conditions,
- Whether in crowded accommodation,
- Quality of diet,
- Ability of parent(s) or guardians to care.

The transit walk is in-depth. It involves going to every household to determine the vulnerable children and vulnerability of the family, with the MVCC establishing an approximate ranking of vulnerability. There is a further step in a democratic and transparent process: the village council calls a meeting at which the information from the transit walk is discussed and debated. This gives an opportunity for members of the community to discuss the fairness and accuracy of the ranking, which may be amended in the light of information that emerges. This leads to a village-level agreement on who needs help and who is suitable for the co-operative. The consent of the community is essential. The first time we set up a co-operative we didn't have the MVCC or the transit walk, and unfortunately an opportunistic individual who was comparatively prosperous was admitted to as a member and used the capital for a project outside the co-op, causing understandable resentment from other members.

Then, based on the list of potential candidates, committee members assess the capacity of individuals of a household to join the agricultural co-op, which is set up in parallel to the MVCC. If a dairy co-op is being set up, the committee will draw up a list of people who are potentially suitable for looking after a cow and joining the enterprise. Then they will recommend to the Ward Steering Committee and the village council a list of around 10 to 20 suitable candidates dependent on the size of the village and nature of the proposed co-op.

The MVCC's work involves a considerable degree of social work. Training covers paralegal and social work training, including issues such as women's and children's rights, and dispute resolution. Each member of the committee visits a caseload on a monthly basis. They monitor the welfare of the children and offer advice to the children and their guardians. After identifying the households in the villages with the most vulnerable children, the Committee develops supporting plans for them.

Africa Bridge supports the Committee with extensive training, focused on understanding the situation of vulnerable children, as well as practical skills such as planning, budgeting and banking. It also provides direct grants for uniforms and shoes to assist children in being able to attend school, and for short-term household needs such as nutrition and shelter. Such direct support is reduced over time and replaced with support from the agricultural co-operatives as they become profitable.

Women in Most Vulnerable Children Committees become

leaders in the community. Within 18 months of the changes we introduced with the first Africa Bridge projects, women were doing much of the talking, and often the chair was a woman. Over the years, we understand that the number of women standing for political positions has increased significantly (see Chapter 8 Women Take a Leading Role).

The co-operative

The Masoko Ward Africa Bridge project was the first to feature an MVCC and ran from 2008-2013. It was a significant success, and we could see the benefits of the twin organizations – the co-op and the MVCC – collaborating closely. The current way of operating in the 2020s adopts a similar approach to this pathfinding project.

The MVCC, with the assistance of Africa Bridge staff, selects the founder members of the agricultural co-op, based on their aptitude and ability as well as the needs of children, in consultation with the local community. We work with the new entities to craft a five-year plan. Africa Bridge staff and the Ward Steering Committee make an assessment for the types of livestock or crop that would be suitable for the village. Obviously, climate, soil quality and terrain are dominant considerations. Tanzania has a tropical climate, but the south west of the country has a cool season in July-August and temperature varies considerably owing to altitude. Chilly nights are not unknown. In the hottest zones, avocado, for example, does not thrive, and here we have opted for chickens or cows. Some potential crops, such as cocoa, are not suitable because of the slow growing time; there would not be a return within the five years of an Africa Bridge project. Typically, there are two to three agricultural co-operatives for each village. Prior to buying any animals or planting crops, there is an intensive training program. This begins with training in governance, financial management and administration, such as running meetings, agreeing decisions and taking minutes. There then follows technical agricultural advice, related to the crop or animal that the co-op selects. Africa Bridge staff work closely with co-operative members to give advice and embed the training and the values of the co-op. They may offer guidance, for example, on chairing meetings; empowerment facilitators may also help in this regard.

Co-ops initially receive a grant from the Africa Bridge organization. In the case of a dairy co-op, Africa Bridge will buy, say, 12 cows and one bull and give them to the 12 founder members of the co-operative. The first calf that is born is donated by each farmer back to the co-op; the second calf is sold, and part of the proceeds go to the Most Vulnerable Children's Committee. Every calf after that belongs to an individual member of the co-operative, who owns the cow and is responsible for taking care of her, but within the context of the co-op membership. They are encouraged to help each other – for example, a members of the co-op may be quite elderly and need help from younger villagers to build a shelter for the cow – but we have found that assigning an individual to each cow fosters a direct sense of responsibility and is more effective in practice. In the case of a co-op with livestock, one or two of the co-op members are trained as nurse practitioners, able to monitor the health of the animals and to know when to call for specialist intervention from a vet. The breed of cow selected will be high-yield and valuable, with registered lineage – some breeds yield significantly more liters of milk per cow than others. There is a market for the calves in Tanzania and a farmer may receive up to $400 for a healthy calf. Manure from the cows is converted to a compost and is used to enhance crop yields for arable produce.

Control of disease is a major issue for agricultural projects. For this reason we adopt 'zero grazing' whereby the cow lives in a cow shelter, and minimal mixing of animals, who are not free to roam and find their own food, as the risk of disease is just too great.

With avocados, the capital payout obviously works differently. Paying back into the co-op the initial loan of 50 seedlings is done in the form of cash, enough to buy 50 seedlings. In addition to the seedlings, members receive some funds for insecticides and fertilizer. As with the dairy co-op, they also make a contribution to the MVCC. As it takes time for an avocado tree to grow and yield fruit, there is a tapered, three-year program for repaying the contractually agreed loan and payments into the MVCC. The first harvest for avocados in year three is pretty small and the trees only reach their prime after 15-20 years. Hence, new avocado co-ops now include chickens to help participants sustain themselves through the early years.

Agricultural produce of the co-ops has included maize, pigs and chickens as well as dairy cows and avocado. Goat co-ops are being piloted in Kambasagela Ward, at the time of writing. Any profits from agricultural assets are reinvested, and new members are encouraged to join. A savings fund is built up to provide loans for emergency needs – for example, taking a child to hospital, or veterinary treatment for a cow – and co-op members receive training on financial accounting and governance.

The general principle is maintained: co-operative members pay back into the co-op so that new members receive agricultural assets. In this way, the co-operative grows in membership and collective wealth, becomes financially generative and self-sufficient, and can grow without further grants from Africa Bridge. It is a profitable local co-operative enterprise that funds the humanitarian work and creates opportunities for children. It is not dependent upon donors.

Each farmer with the co-op is an individual entrepreneur. We find that this approach encourages a deep engagement with the project, and creates an incentive for economic growth and development, including diversification. So, while they are part of a co-op, the co-operative element is limited to a savings fund with loan facilities and contributions to help vulnerable children. Once an individual has repaid their loans and made their contractual payments to the MVCC, they are free to retain profits, improve quality of life for their families, and reinvest as they judge appropriate.

. . .

Development and growth

The Africa Bridge approach encourages a mindset of entrepreneurialism and growth, such that the co-ops add members and scale, both during the five years of establishing the programs and subsequently. The concept is one of sustainable growth and supporting the children and rest of the community, not scaling up as an end in itself.

As mentioned, while there is a co-operative element, the individual farmer is free to retain profits and reinvest, should they choose, after repaying loans and contributing to the MVCC and the savings fund. Some have expanded their businesses, often with great success. For example, some avocado farmers from Africa Bridge co-operatives formed an association, including non-Africa Bridge farmers, and identified four buyers for the UK market. They expanded their sales, including exports, with the achieved price rising from 390 Shillings per kilo to 1,250 Shillings within a few years, transforming their business's fortunes and the quality of life for their families. In a similar initiative in Rungwe, Africa Bridge dairy farmers pooled resources for storage and refrigeration facilities and negotiated to become suppliers for a yoghurt company. I was on an internal flight and received a yoghurt produced with milk from this enterprise as part of the in-flight meal. I felt quite emotional with pride.

Other examples of diversification include setting up retail and hospitality outlets, a corn-milling service, a community bank, and a rental service for a commercial rotavator for farmers. Not all enterprises flourished – that is a feature of entrepreneurialism anywhere in the world – but a great number have, as the case studies featured throughout this book demonstrate. Through setting up and running their own small business, individuals have developed skills, confidence, and entrepreneurial flair that enable both diversification and recovery from setbacks. For example, one co-operative was running a pig farm that was affected by swine flu. We started five pig co-ops in Isongole Ward between 2005 and 2007, but all the pigs died or were destroyed due to swine flu in 2010. That business was ruined, but within a short space of time some co-operative members had established different businesses. One member had built a home and learned business skills. She opened a pub and two shops that were soon thriving. All her children were attending school.

Handover and assessment

Consistent with the principle of being self-sustaining and generative, the direct involvement of Africa Bridge staff and funds is time limited. After five years the charity's employees withdraw from the project, handing over a sustainable set of projects, which in practice has tended to continue to grow and develop, sometimes becoming the center of a cluster of enterprises.

At the end of five years the Ward has 'graduated' and Africa Bridge withdraws its support. The handover in reality is an ongoing process throughout the last three years. However, at the end of year five a closing contract is signed by all parties stating what their responsibilities are in the future. For example, each co-op member signs a contract on Day 1 of their joining which commits them to pass on assets. The Ward and village governments are expected to make sure these pass-ons continue in the co-ops. The co-ops continue and each co-op member, after meeting the pass-on commitments, is an independent entrepreneur who happens to be a member of a co-op.

Africa Bridge has always monitored the effectiveness of each five-year co-operative program. There is a baseline survey at the start, and a final survey. Indicators include: meals per day, savings, household possessions, quality of housing, numbers of children in school, whether there is a medical plan. Key to developing the strength of the model has been to create partnerships between the Most Vulnerable Children's Committees and the agricultural co-ops. The former defines and monitors the social goals, the latter provides the income and other resources to fulfil them.

KEY POINTS

- Children are the first to speak in discussions that are preparatory to setting up an Africa Bridge project. This inverts a conventional approach to economic development, but has been highly effective in our experience.
- When children are the initial focus, this often leads to an open and transparent conversation that yields important and challenging information about social issues. Sensitive issues arise that require skilled facilitation.
- Three key organizations are set up to implement an Africa Bridge project: a Ward Steering Committee for the whole ward, a Most Vulnerable Children's Committee for each village, and up to three agricultural co-operatives per village. There is careful selection for membership.
- Key to the establishment of the MVCCs and the co-operatives is intensive training in all disciplines, ranging from social work to administration and technical agricultural expertise.
- The co-operatives comprise individual farmers, able to retain a proportion of their profits, and diversify and grow should they choose. Many have done so to considerable effect.
- After five years, Africa Bridge staff withdraw from the project, leaving a cluster of viable businesses.
- There is an assessment of social outcomes at the end of five years, compared against a baseline taken at the beginning. Improving the outcomes for most vulnerable children is always the guiding aim.
- Committees must comprise at least 50% women. There has been a considerable increase in empowerment of

women in the areas where Africa Bridge projects have been established.

PART TWO

FINDINGS FROM AFRICA BRIDGE AND IMPLICATIONS

CHAPTER 4
AFRICA BRIDGE
EFFECTIVENESS
FINDINGS FROM THE KISONDELA SURVEY

The Kisondela Ward comprises six villages in southwestern Tanzania: Bugoba, Isuba, Kibatata, Lutetde, Mpuga, and Ndubi. According to the 2012 national census, they together had a population of 11,070. They are situated in the Rungwe district, Mbeya Region, close to the border with Malawi and Zambia. The geography is partially forested and fairly mountainous, near to Rungwe Mountain, the third highest in Tanzania, with a summit of 2,981 meters.

The ward was selected in accordance with the process described in Chapter 3 How Africa Bridge Operates, as being characterized by high levels of extreme poverty and potential for the development of agricultural co-operatives. It was the fifth Africa Bridge project. The baseline survey identified 1,346 most vulnerable children in 635 households. Some of the indicators of poverty and distress in the baseline study included: 95% of households reporting food shortages, 32% living in a home with grass roof, some 95% of children sleeping on a mat on the ground. Extreme poverty was cited as a problem with regards to caring for children by 74% of respondents.

The Kisondela Africa Bridge program ran from 2016-2021. It featured a dairy co-operative, chicken farming and cultivation of avocado, for each of the six villages. In mid-2021 an end-project survey was carried out in line with our regular practice – for all previous Africa Bridge projects we had conducted a baseline, and end survey. For the first time in the history of Africa Bridge, an external specialist research agency, MarketShare Associates, was hired to conduct the survey. The report was completed in September 2021.

Researchers verified that the Kisondela population suffers from more extreme poverty than the average for rural Tanzania. Findings from the research showed significant, potentially life-changing improvements for many households from this low base in the communities participating in the Africa Bridge program over the five-year period. In particular, the survey found major improvements to living conditions, savings and assets, and reduction in hunger and extreme poverty. Key findings include:

- Extreme poverty cited as a problem in caring for children reduced from 74% to 46%.
- The proportion of families reporting food shortages fell from 95% of households, to 33%.
- The proportion owning livestock increased by 300%.
- The number of households with most vulnerable children who eat three meals per day rose from 16% at baseline to 52% in 2021.
- Quality of housing improved radically for a large proportion of participants.
- The number of families able to save money rose from four to 104.

Sample population and methods
A baseline wellbeing survey was carried out in Kisondela Ward in 2016, as co-operatives were being formed. It included a sample of

355 out of 635 households, selected according to who had received initial support from Africa Bridge in the form of cows, chickens, or avocado tree saplings. The same sample size was used for a mini survey that Africa Bridge conducted in 2018. The endline survey aimed to interview the same households, ultimately including a total of 343 households.

The endline survey was carried out in July and August 2021. The five-year period of direct Africa Bridge involvement in the co-operatives and MVCCs had come to an end in March 2021. The field research team consisted of two pairs consisting of an interviewer and a data recorder. They carried out interviews with households and recorded the data on Kobo Toolbox software. Informed consent of the respondent was obtained for the survey at the start of the interview. The respondent was given the option to 1) not participate, 2) not answer any question during the interview, and 3) stop at any time.

The study is overwhelmingly quantitative, recording key indicators of poverty and well-being, comparing data in 2021 with that collected for the baseline survey five years earlier. There are plans by Africa Bridge to incorporate more qualitative studies in the future, which will help identify causal links: which interventions are the most effective in enhancing wellbeing and opportunities for most vulnerable children and in reducing poverty.

Findings in detail

The findings are grouped into five categories: Nutrition, Housing, Household Income and Assets, Education and Skills, and Business Development. The categories overlap to a significant extent, given the interrelationships of these factors both in the dynamics of poverty, and the dynamics of moving out of poverty. Examples include: improved diet and housing improves health; better physical living conditions encourage the ability to study, improving education and ability to earn; stronger cash income and ability to save increases options for reinvestment and business development.

Some of the most striking improvements were to the quality of housing, lighting and clothing. Clearly, such features were a priority for many of the families. This demonstrates the importance of physical comfort to quality of life and as a foundation for further improving a family's prospects. It is also a reflection of the very low starting point, with households experiencing severe deprivation at the point of the baseline survey, sleeping on a mat on a floor in almost all cases, and many with a roof of thatch and a floor of mud.

1 Nutrition and health

There were some notable shifts in diet, some of which were difficult to interpret without qualitative data. For example, there was a fall in consumption of beans and lentils, but a significant increase in the use of both green leafy vegetables and yellow and orange vegetables. Overall, though, diet appears to have improved significantly, with a huge fall in the proportion of households reporting food shortages – from 95% to 33% – and there was a wider variety of food consumed, researchers found. Perhaps the most encouraging finding was that the proportion of households with most vulnerable children eating three meals per day rose dramatically from 16% at baseline to 52% in 2021.

Lack of land for producing food and low yields were cited as the main problems in 2021. This compares with low yields and lack of money as the principal barriers in 2016. Financial constraints fell from 24% to 12% as a reason for food shortages.

There was an improvement in access to water, with 70% taking less than half an hour to collect water, compared with 57% at baseline; and there was an increase from 3% to 7% in homes accessing water via their own tap. The proportion taking an hour or more to collect water fell from 9% to 1%. Some 94% of households were not using a water purification process, but this may reflect good quality of source water from a spring or well.

On health, just 12% of those surveyed have health insurance, but this is an increase from only 1% in 2016. In 2021 some 54% of most vulnerable children had a birth certificate, up from 16% five years earlier.

2 Housing

In 2016 some 32% of households had a grass roof; this fell to zero five years later, by which time all roofs were metal, or mixed metal and thatch. The number of families using cement bricks rose from four to 85, while the proportion with a cement floor rose from 9% to 34%, with a fall in the incidence of dirt floors from 75% to 63% (some floors were mixed mud and cement).

Use of a separate cooking area rose from 75% to 85%. The significance of this is that cooking methods often include heating food over a fire or a kerosene stove, so a separate area reduces inhalation of smoke, which is helpful to health.

The proportion of residents with home lighting increased from 7% to 45%. This is a factor in the ability of a child to study.

There was a slight improvement to toilet facilities, with an increasing number having a cement floor for their latrine (from 3% to 9%), and a small number able to have a flush toilet (3%, up from 2%).

3 Household income and asset ownership

Financial security and prospects improved sharply for many of the survey respondents. A total of 30% reported being able to save money, up from just 1% at baseline. Ability to earn income from selling dairy produce was reported by 22%, compared with zero in 2016, while the proportion earning from the sale of crops increased from 51% to 69%. These findings clearly reflect the impact of the agricultural co-operatives. The proportion earning money from wages fell slightly. Just 2% had a bank account, up from zero five years earlier; however, this is an indicator of diminishing significance in rural Tanzania because electronic payments via cellphones have increased sharply and do not require the user to have a bank account. In this way many businesspeople and individuals have leapfrogged economies with higher rates of bank account usage, deploying a more technologically advanced and efficient payment system.

Ownership of livestock increased substantially. Chickens were owned by 92% of respondents, compared with 52% in 2016; the proportion owning cows increased from 25% to 67%.

The number of households able to buy domestic items also increased. For example, the proportion owning a table rose from 59% to 71%, and cellphone ownership increased in similar fashion, from 45% to 69%.

Cellphone ownership is even more significant and empowering in rural Tanzania than in most parts of the world, because other elements of communications infrastructure are typically absent or inadequate. There are few TVs, no broadband – often not even electricity. Cellphones are powered through solar-powered chargers and have given thousands of Tanzanians access to the internet and mobile banking. For farmers and other entrepreneurs, this is life-changing; they can check the spot prices for crops and cattle in the trading centers, making them less vulnerable to over-charging by middlemen, and they can send and receive electronic payment, which offers more convenience and security than cash. Most banks have been slow to offer accounts to those in rural areas, but some of the more innovative banking institutions have partnered with network providers to enable electronic payment to those without a bank account. Possession of a cellphone and a solar charger can be life changing. A solar charger can also be used to power a light for reading, studying, and doing accounts in the evening, as well as powering the phone. Access to such relatively inexpensive devices can be decisive in being able to run a business. A brief overview and recent history of the socioeconomic reality of Tanzania is given in Chapter 6.

Other major improvements in household assets included a large increase in the proportion sleeping on a mattress (up from just 5% to 38%) and an improvement in the proportion of children with a sweater (15% to 79%). These investments are in the same vein as emphasis on improvements to the standard of housing: a clear desire to improve comfort and dignity at home, from a low starting point, having the side-effect of providing a foundation for further improvements to quality of life, such as the ability to study.

4 Educational opportunities

There was a significant increase in attendance at secondary school, from 9% to 32%. In part this reflects the natural ageing of the sample population over the five years, but the proportion in primary school also stayed at a healthy level. Most encouragingly, the proportion of children not attending school for financial reasons fell from 13% to 2%.

The sharp increase in proportion of households with lighting, up to nearly half from just above zero, improves the environment in which children study. Moreover, the greater number of children with sweaters also potentially improves comfort when studying, as evenings in this part of Tanzania can be chilly in the winter owing to the altitude.

5 Skills and business development

Researchers found that reinvestment of savings was notable. They chronicled a total of 22 investments by the sample population, including seven in chicken farming. Interestingly, there were two examples of investments in pig farming, even though pigs were not featured in the agricultural co-operatives set up by Africa Bridge in

Kisondela. Such entrepreneurial diversification was also noted in participants in earlier Africa Bridge programs, and strongly supports a conclusion that the initiative can boost business skills generally, helping to spawn a cluster of successful businesses.

Observations by MarketShare

MarketShare is a global consulting company (https://market shareassociates.com/), specializing in research and advice on economic development, especially in deprived regions. Their staff are familiar with a range of different types of projects aimed at reducing poverty and improving life prospects in different regions around the world. Many of these programs are agricultural. In carrying out this research, they were able to bring independence, a high degree of academic rigor, and an ability to benchmark against other development programs.

In addition to the specific findings, the researchers made four general conclusions from their observations and research:

- The base population in the Kisondela Ward are **exceptionally and multi-dimensionally deprived,** by national standards. MarketShare's assessment concluded that the proportion of the local population experiencing severe poverty was 75%, compared with a rural average of 50% and 49% for the whole of Tanzania. It used the internationally recognized Multidimensional Poverty Index (MPI), which was developed by Oxford Poverty and Human Development Initiative with the UN Development Program (UNDP). The index assesses factors such as the incidence and intensity of poverty and the proportion of the population that is multidimensionally poor.
- The **vast majority of indicators of wellbeing improved** over the five years of the program. The incidence of

extreme poverty, food shortages and lack of basic housing amenities, among many other indicators, fell appreciably, as noted in the findings.

- The **levels of reinvestment** were noteworthy and encouraging. Researchers identified some 22 examples of reinvestment, including examples of entrepreneurial diversification.
- The Africa Bridge model **appears to be unique** in its combination of features, although some of the elements are to be found in other programs. Agricultural co-operatives are widespread across the world, and the graduation model, popularized by BRAC in Bangladesh, also seeks to achieve 'pathways out of poverty'. Similarities between graduation models and Africa Bridge are: spatial mapping to identify the poorest households; providing an asset (typically agricultural); training individuals and providing healthcare support. Differences are that Africa Bridge requires participants to pass on an asset (see Chapter 3), and that while savings models are an explicit part of the graduation model, they are not in Africa Bridge (although many Africa Bridge programs have featured savings arrangements). The focus on most vulnerable children does appear in other approaches, but is a particularly strong and central feature of the Africa Bridge approach.

MarketShare has produced literature on the graduation model approach.[1]

Recommendations for future surveys

One recommendation of the report is to incorporate more quali-tative questions as part of future surveys, to discover more about the drivers of change. Some indications of this emerged from the

2021 survey, regarding for example the source of income for house-holds and how they had altered. Other findings were intriguing, and called for further inquiry: for example, into the decrease in consumption of pulses and the increase in vegetables.

Qualitative findings – The quantitative findings from the 2021 survey reveal much about what has changed. Qualitative findings can yield greater insights into *why*. This helps test the Theory of Change, so as to better indicate which features of the agricultural co-operatives and the Most Vulnerable Children's Committees, and coordination between the two, were most helpful. This would help inform further reform to the approach.

Monitoring against comparators and against time – Measuring the Multidimensional Poverty Indicator in comparison with a sample population not participating in an Africa Bridge program would give greater clarity and depth of knowledge as to causal factors. Monitoring against time – MarketShare recommended year-on-year assessments – helps assure program directors that the approach is broadly effective. This could pick up, for example, a dip or reversal in the rate of poverty reduction, or sudden improvement, with qualitative surveys then able to discern the likely reasons.

Researchers noted that sustainability, both of the institutions and of the moves out of poverty, is a key indicator. In particular, it would be helpful to monitor the extent to which improvements are sustained significantly beyond the end of the five-year period. This would need to be a multidimensional assessment, including open-ended and other qualitative questions. For example, the end of a particular co-operative venture may not represent a failure if it was superseded by different successful ventures, with continued enhancement to earnings and prospects.

SUMMARY

Independent verification of the overwhelmingly positive trend in the reduction of extreme poverty, and the opening up of opportunities for families participating in Africa Bridge programs in the Kisondela ward, is tremendously encouraging. This applies both to those directly benefiting and potentially to many more, given that this evidence base provides a foundation for introducing the program to many other regions, fine-tuning the approach in the light of these and future findings. The results from the research are similar to endline surveys produced by Africa Bridge staff in earlier programs, the difference on this occasion being that they have been independently verified by experienced and highly qualified researchers who are able to draw comparisons with other approaches.

CHAPTER 5
THEORY OF CHANGE AND EMERGING PRINCIPLES

There is an old quip about professional economists, being the kind of experts who can explain to you tomorrow why the things they predicted yesterday did not occur today. Economic and social life is unpredictable. There are too many variables and unscripted events for it to be modellable in a reliable way.

This does not mean, however, that we cannot apply evidence and some rigor to our approaches in order to attain better outcomes, as I hope the findings from the previous chapter demonstrate.

Collectively, humans can be slow learners. In social programs, we are capable of humane and evidence-based learning to guide and steadily improve programs that bring a lasting benefit to societies. In practice, there are many ways in which such progress becomes inhibited. One dimension is psychological: individual ego, the 'not invented here' syndrome, and misplaced motives. Another is the difficulty of assessing what works in complex systems – confusing correlation for causation, for example.

A common criticism of an approach that aspires to be evidence-based in the complex economic and social world is that 'there's only a correlation between the apparent good practices and the good outcomes that we measure'. This observation is often true, yet not always helpful. It has been stated in a way that implies two misleading beliefs: that a 100% proof of causality is achievable and infinitely repeatable (it typically isn't), and that the presence of a strong and consistent correlation is not important (it generally is). If there is a strong and consistent correlation between certain practices and better social outcomes as measured by quantitative data – in our context, matters such as better nutrition, school attendance and literacy – then it makes sense to continue those practices, while simultaneously experimenting with other approaches that also hold promise, and continuing to measure the impacts and make rational comparisons to deepen our understanding of probable causal factors.

Management of organizations and social enterprises involves choice. If you are pursuing a certain course of action, you are rejecting others. The strategies chosen may 'only' be based on correlations and the balance of probabilities, but this may mean that it is the best course of action, often by a considerable margin. Sometimes the balance of probabilities weighs so heavily in favor of certain practices that it would be irrational to reject them. For example, we have learned that the survival rate of Most Vulnerable Children's Committees after several years is close to 100% when there is a comprehensive training program for founders and participants, and that the survival rate is close to 0% when there is minimal training and preparation. The importance of long-term preparation and commitment is discussed further in Chapter 7 There Are No Shortcuts.

Social scientists have grappled with the dilemmas around correlation, causality and the behavior of complex systems for decades, and there is increasing understanding of how to make rational, evidence-based choices. The 'it's only a correlation' objection is becoming obsolete, replaced by a sophisticated approach that accepts complexity and acknowledges that a 100% consistent linear-cause-and-effect proof, that may work for physical sciences in a laboratory, is not always replicable in a social setting. Such a pragmatic approach is multi-disciplinary, delves into complexity, and reduces the amount of guesswork involved, increasing the level of certainty. It integrates three approaches: the quantitative study (what happens – the outcomes), the qualitative study (analysis of questionnaire-based surveys that indicate why things are happening) and case study material (stories that yield further insights into the causal dynamics). While this book is not a formal textbook, I have sought to present what we have discovered in all three dimensions, in association with our research partners.

For Africa Bridge, our academic partners have developed a Theory of Change that was developed in the light of experience from the first two decades, drawing in particular on their study in 2021. The Theory of Change is a form of causal architecture that explains the likely impact of different elements within the model. It posits that certain inputs – such as facilitators, paralegal training, and resources such as school uniforms and agricultural equipment – can be combined and coordinated to produce direct effects – such as strong forms of collaboration and agricultural skills and greater economic activity – that in turn yield multiple and sustainable social benefits (see diagram).

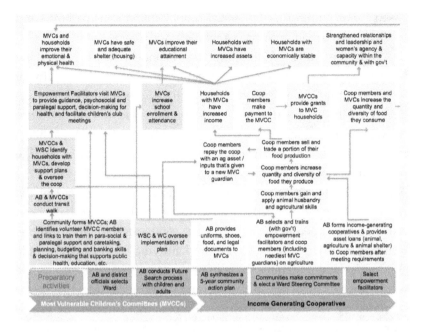

Our research partners identify two likely causal drivers of improved social and health outcomes: the Most Vulnerable Children's Committees and the Income-Generating Co-operatives. These underlie multiple identified probable lines of causality that explain certain outcomes. For example, providing grants to households with most vulnerable children for uniforms, food, housing and legal documents leads to higher school attendance, leading to better educational outcomes. Another is setting up agricultural co-operatives, which leads to better supply of food and more varied diet, which in turn leads to other outcomes – namely, better diet for households directly benefitting and more opportunities to enhance household income, leading to better quality of life and improved economic stability. The Theory of Change diagram includes multiple lines of causality. These are both in parallel – some initiatives have multiple consequences – and sequential – some build strengths which in turn build further strengths and benefits. The approach is based upon building the social and economic capability and resilience of the community as a whole.

While the study in 2021 into the Kisondela Ward, headed by MarketShare Associates and Dr Heath Prince of the University of Texas, was the first independent academic survey into the effectiveness of Africa Bridge, it was not by any means the first survey. Since we were founded in 2000, we have been continually testing, checking, surveying and interviewing. Each five-year Africa Bridge program has featured a baseline survey and an end-survey. In 2019 I made a visit to all Africa Bridge projects to make a record of the results and the most effective initiatives. Several practices have been refined or scrapped in the light of what we discovered. For example, bringing more rigor to the means of identifying the most vulnerable children or strengthening the role of the Ward Steering Committee were reforms whose initiation and continued practice were informed by feedback and survey findings, not intuition or guesswork. My background is in total quality management, so I was schooled in the discipline of continuous improvement, informed by continual measurement of outcomes for the end customer.

In the following chapters, we will discuss in more depth some of the most probable significant causal factors behind the improvements that we and our research partners have recorded. In line with the observation made earlier, that management is about choice, and about selecting the better alternative. This book also records some of the lessons learned from some of the ventures that either did not work, had difficult unexpected consequences, or were sub-optimal. For example, the co-operatives had a bigger impact when closely linked with the Most Vulnerable Children's Committees, the role of facilitators appeared to help significantly, and so on. This is discussed further in Chapter 9 Continual Learning.

Overall, we have discerned certain general findings:

What fails – remote decision-making, insufficient training and preparation, asymmetry of opportunities causing division in the community, motivation based solely on financial returns for asset owners.

What works – local group decision-making, patient building of both technical skills and community cohesion, equality of input, motivation based on outcomes for vulnerable children and entrepreneurial opportunities for farmers, building on strengths rather than trying to solve problems. Identifying children as the core beneficiaries is effective in multiple ways: it strengthens the future prospects for the community, it is a unifying objective, and it lessens political tension, as children are not asset-owners.

How we know – The above were initial discoveries, empirical and from some survey results. By 2020 we were increasingly confident of the ingredients of success for the Africa Bridge approach. We experience it as: 1) transfer of commitment from Africa Bridge to the community, 2) generative energy, 3) sustainability. Effectiveness is understood as eradication of extreme poverty and improvement of life prospects for the whole community in a sustainable and equitable fashion.

SUMMARY

The Theory of Change, while being subject to further evaluation, is already based upon evidence, from the continual internal surveys carried out by Africa Bridge staff and volunteers in the project's first 20 years, further confirmed by independent academic findings. The strategic purpose of Africa Bridge is to lift communities out of poverty with a model that is sustainable and equitable; also, one that is low-cost and scalable. The Theory of Change model shows the causal links that demonstrate how this model, which we can say with increasing confidence is proven in practice, works at the level of the community.

PART THREE
IMPLICATIONS OF THE AFRICA BRIDGE EXPERIENCE

The following chapters discuss some of the most significant themes from our research findings in more depth:

- Building on inherent strengths, rooted in the culture of Tanzania.
- The importance of long-term and in-depth training.
- Giving women a leading role.
- Continual learning.
- The importance of love, passion and purpose.

CHAPTER 6
CONTEXT
AN OVERVIEW OF THE CULTURE AND
GEOGRAPHY OF TANZANIA

'We, the people of Tanganyika,
 would like to light a candle on top of Mount Kilimanjaro,
 which would shine beyond our borders,
 giving hope where there was despair,
 love where there was hate
 and dignity where before there was only humiliation.......
 We cannot, unlike other countries, send rockets to the moon,
 but we can send rockets of love and hope
 to our fellow men wherever they may be'
 President Julius Nyerere, First President of Tanzania.
 9 December 1961

Every year in Tanzania there is a nationwide event, known as the Uhuru Torch rally, somewhat akin to the journey of the Olympic torch in the host nation of the games. It takes place over the course of several weeks, and the ceremonial bronze torch is carried alternately by runners and by vehicles (it is a large country), taking a different route each year, ensuring that different regions are progressively covered over the course of time. During the tour, officials inspect construction projects or lay foundation stones, incorporating a practical element into an otherwise symbolic ritual. The culmination of the rally is a ceremony on 14 October, Nyerere Day. The symbol of a light shining is borrowed directly from the late President's poem about lighting a candle and sending 'rockets of love', to remind citizens of the transformative power of caring about citizens; neighbors and strangers alike. The reference to Mount Kilimanjaro reflected a desire to shine a metaphorical beacon to the whole world, from Africa's highest point.

Every Tanzanian citizen is familiar with the text of President Nyerere's poem, and the torch procession is a major national event. It has at times attracted criticism for becoming large and expensive, with many public officials taking part. Nonetheless, it is striking that a nation should have an iconic national event that features a symbol of love rather than of military conquest or an independence campaign, more typically commemorated in national days of cele-bration around the world.

The ceremony of the torch reflects a national culture that takes pride in being welcoming and hospitable. Mathayo Mwakagamba is a Tanzanian architect who is a friend of Africa Bridge. He is from the Rungwe region of southwest Tanzania, where Africa Bridge has run its projects to date, but is based in Dar es Salaam, the country's largest city, where his business is based. He describes how the concept of hospitality is central to Tanzanian culture, so that trav-elers will think well of the community that has accepted them. He says:

'Whenever we see a stranger, somebody who is a foreigner, we normally tend to be very welcoming. And very humble. Whatever we do, he will actually go back at his home and ... [report that] Tanzanians are very humble people. Whenever we see a stranger, we tend to be more generous, more humble, as soon as we know that person is not from here.'

In keeping with the spirit of hospitality there is a strong tendency in Tanzania to soften and ameliorate religious and political viewpoints, rather than coalesce behind an ideological line. There

are few, if any, strident sects or movements. There are no book burn-
ings or demagogic preachers. One can observe an instinctive, collective desire to humanize and moderate. The culture is polite, at times
to a fault, as there can be a tendency to defer to an authority figure
where it might be reasonable to challenge; but on the whole the
capacity to adapt, soften and be pragmatic rather than be rigid or
ideological is an asset. For example, when we as the founders of
Africa Bridge challenged the idea that men should hold all positions
of authority, and expressed the intention to have equal gender representation, this request was accommodated without any significant
opposition.

Modern history and influence of culture

While it is difficult to do justice to something as complex as
national culture – there is always the risk of simplifying or stereo-
typing complex social realities – there are marked differences
between Tanzania and neighboring countries. It is helpful to understand and work with a society's prevailing values and mores when
one is involved in economic and social development programs.

The culture of pragmatism, politeness and hospitality has
shaped the nation's politics as much as its exposure to economic and
political ideas, perhaps more so. For decades, up until the early
1960s, Tanzania was governed by external powers. Since independence, a single party has dominated Tanzanian politics. The
Tanganyikan African National Union (TANU) was founded in 1954
by Julius Nyerere, who was to become the independent nation's first
president. In 1977 TANU merged with the Afro-Shirazi Party, the
principal party of Zanzibar, to form Chama Cha Mapinduzi (CCM),
which remains the ruling party at the time of writing. In effect
Tanzania operates as a one-party state, although in 1992 the constitution was amended to permit other legal political parties[1].)

Although it has been a one-party state for many decades,
Tanzania has not been affected by significant levels of repression or

corruption often associated with one-party states, and many local government officials are committed to social and economic development. While there is some crime and corruption, as with all nations, generally the levels of personal safety are good. Nevertheless, there are resentments about a single party being in power for such a long time, with suspicions that elections are not fair.[2]

Nyerere, who died in 1999, was an African independence campaigner. He was a committed socialist and nationalized many industries. In keeping with Tanzanian culture, he was moderate and pragmatic. He had been influenced by Mahatma Ghandi's philosophy of non-violence and fostered national unity. Ideologically, he could be seen to be similar in outlook to Nelson Mandela. He remains widely respected in Tanzania today, and is often known as Mwalimu, or Teacher. The annual Uhuru torch rally is one of several ways that his legacy is honored.

The Arusha Declaration of 1967 defined the philosophy of TANU (as it then was), committing it to economic self-reliance and a socialist economic model as the nation moved away from colonialist rule, as well as to human rights such as freedom of expression and religious belief[3]. By the 21st Century there was little in the way of socialist-style central planning, and a mixed economy had become established, with many thriving businesses.

When Nyerere came to power in the 1960s, the challenge he faced was more of building a nation than of overseeing regime change. Tanzania had around 100 tribes and had been governed by external powers for a long period. The sheer number of relatively small ethnic groupings had an advantage in that a single tribe did not dominate, as has occurred in other African nations, resulting in inequalities, resentments and, in some cases, conflict. Nyerere's policies were not without fault; an early experiment to relocate people from their home village to another, in order to mix tribes and lessen rivalries, caused some upset, as people resented being moved. As a pragmatist, however, he dropped the policy. In a similarly pragmatic way, while he sought to move decisively towards economic independence and a break from colonial admin-istration, he did not dismiss all individuals who worked for the previous regime. He decided to retain my father, for example, as an agricultural adviser for some two years after independence. Nyerere took a genuine interest in agriculture and valued my father's ability.

In March 2021 Samia Suhulu Hassan became Tanzania's first female President, stepping up from her role as Vice President after President John Magufuli died. She has been noted for her more pragmatic approach to dealing with the Covid epidemic. She curbed larger gatherings and encouraged Tanzanians to get vaccinated, reversing the policy of her predecessor and publicly getting the jab herself in July 2021[4].

Geography and demographics

Tanzania is a sub-Saharan African country with a tropical climate, in the southern hemisphere. It was formed in 1964 as a fully independent country, having seceded from the British Empire, comprising the continental nation of Tanganyika and the former island state of Zanzibar in the Indian ocean, close to the Tanzanian mainland. Tanganyika had already been granted effective autonomy under the British crown in 1961.

It features the world-famous sites of Mount Kilimanjaro, the highest mountain in Africa, and the Serengeti wildlife reserve, both in the north of the country near the border with Kenya. It is a fairly large country at 945,000 km^2, about the same size as Texas and New Mexico combined. Dar es Salaam is the largest city with a popula-tion of around 7 million, and is a major port on the Indian Ocean. Tanga is another significant port, located in the north of the country. Major inland cities include Arusha, Mwanza (on the south shore of Lake Victoria), Dodoma and Mbeya. Officially Dodoma is the capi-tal, but Dar es Salaam is the principal commercial center.

Major religions are Christianity and Islam, with a high concentration of Muslims on the island of Zanzibar and in the coastal region. There are also traditional religions.

Infrastructure and economic development

In the early years of Africa Bridge, the infrastructure – electricity, internet access, banking and so on – was very limited. Since the 1990s there has been some improvements in investment in health-care and education, supported by the state, and also by international NGOs, philanthropic corporations such as Abbott Foundation, and the international US President's emergency program to fight HIV/AIDS (PEPFAR). There have also been concerted efforts to improve infrastructure, for example connecting all towns and villages to electrical supplies, with investment in the Rural Energy Authority.

Mathayo Mwakagamba reports that the marginal cost of adding a new property to the grid has fallen to just 27,000 shillings, or around $10, so many more are becoming connected. As an architect with domestic and commercial projects in different parts of the country, he has first-hand experience of how this has affected the construction industry. In the past, many projects in rural areas were hampered as the region was off-grid. He says: 'They were missing electricity supplies, so they had to travel with generators to make sure that the tools for cutting and for welding and whatever during constructions [were connected] ... So we were getting some prob-lems during construction. But nowadays so many areas have elec-tricity supplies, so we don't have a problem during construction. So after design, we are sure of getting a high quality building because of tools working properly because they're connected.'

Improvement to the infrastructure is having a positive effect on economic development generally, as more homes and businesses are connected to mains electricity and wi-fi, he reports.

•   •   •

Demographics and health

The population of Tanzania has increased approximately five-fold since the 1950s, at a greater rate than economic growth or agricultural productivity, putting a strain on food resources. Urban populations increased sharply, with the population of Dar es Salaam rising to around 7 million, compared with less than half a million at independence. Poverty remains a serious problem, especially in rural areas. However, many social and health indicators have shown steady improvement since the late 20th Century. The proportion of those in extreme poverty, defined as an income of US $1.90 or less, has approximately halved, but from a very high starting point. It fell from over 80% to 47% between 2000 and 2019[5].

Life expectancy at birth was very low until the early 21st Century. It was just 43 in 1960, rose steadily to the low-50s over succeeding decades, but then dipped during the AIDS epidemic in the late 1990s from 51 to 49. By 2019, however, it had risen to 65, according to the World Bank[6]. A significant factor within this improvement has been improved maternal care and sharply reduced infant mortality, from a shocking level of 25% in 1960, to 5% in 2019[7]. Deaths from malnutrition, defined as premature deaths due to protein-energy deficiency, fell from 40 per 100,000 to 15 in the period 1990 to 2019[8].

These indicators are averages, and it is possible that data on which health statistics are prepared is skewed towards the urban populations where there is more access to hospitals and clinics, and that the health indicators are lagging in some rural areas. Nonetheless, there have undoubtedly been improvements in the first decades of the 21st Century, in the key areas of maternal care, infant health and curbing the impact of AIDS. There have been significant falls in extreme poverty but from a very high starting point and it remains a serious problem.

In the early 21st Century affordable treatments for AIDS became more available throughout Africa, with the help of a major investment program initiated by the then US President George W Bush, initially in partnership with Kofi Annan, the then Secretary General of the United Nations. This resulted in a health project known as PEPFAR (President's Emergency Plan for AIDS Relief), with a budget totaling tens of billions of dollars between 2001 and 2008, mostly in sub-Saharan Africa. It had a major impact. As well as paying for affordable medication, investment covered training of healthcare professionals and equipping clinics, as well as public health education programs. In addition to the direct benefit for affected patients, access to treatment encouraged individuals to be tested[9].

Education

The TANU government, shortly after independence, established Swahili as the official language, to instill an element of national unity, to aid educational programs and literacy, and to help trade and development. Swahili is the language used in primary schools; only a few elderly people are mono-lingual in their local tongue. The language is widely spoken, with UNESCO estimating that over 200 million people speak the language worldwide, particularly in central and eastern regions of sub-Saharan Africa. It has official status in Kenya and Tanzania. English is also widely spoken, for example among teachers, academics and international businesspeople.

School enrolment statistics from the World Bank show a near threefold improvement, from 34% gross to 96%, in the period 1970-2019[10]. The literacy rate is 77%, up from 59% in 1988. It is 73% for women and 83% for men[11]. In my experience, there is an exceptionally high regard for the value of education among Tanzanians, and remaining barriers to schooling and literacy are to do with lack of resources or access. Caring and domestic responsibilities are often a significant burden for women and girls who wish to be educated and gain access to training and employment.

SUMMARY

Inherent strengths of Tanzanian society

For a project such as Africa Bridge it is important to understand the context in-depth, in order to acknowledge both the inherent strengths and the obstacles to economic and social development. A strong ethos that values education and enterprise, together with a strong agricultural tradition and knowledge, and close community bonds and extended families, represent some of the latent potential that Africa Bridge has sought to build upon. There has also been internal peace for an extended period and strong public administration.

While there have been instances of corruption and fraud, there are also dedicated public servants capable of forming productive partnerships with NGOs, and there have been investments by the state in education, health and other public services. The data that Africa Bridge can present in terms of significant improvements in health indicators and reduced poverty can be used by local politicians to demonstrate progress to central government agencies, who in turn can inform international bodies such as the United Nations.

Tanzanians are generally a polite, welcoming and friendly people, a factor which has greatly assisted the founders of Africa Bridge as we have sought to establish a relationship of trust, to convince people we are committed to the long haul, and to engage in the co-creation of successful enterprises and programs to overcome poverty. Mathayo Mwakagamba pays Africa Bridge a glowing compliment when he says that: 'What Nyerere says about love and hope to our fellow men, that is what Africa Bridge is doing for the orphans, those living in difficult conditions. That is what Mwalimu Nyerere was trying to achieve. He was trying as much as possible to ensure that living conditions for all Tanzanians were improving. So basically that is the approach of Africa Bridge.'

Identifying strengths in a community or individuals, rather than focusing exclusively on weaknesses or gaps, tends to accelerate progress. There are inherent strengths within the rural villages of Tanzania in which we operate: people have a long-established agricultural knowledge and heritage. There is strong community care; for example, there are no homeless children – an orphan will typically be taken in by another family.

CHAPTER 7
THERE ARE NO SHORTCUTS

"The more I practise, the luckier I get," – Gary Player, former champion golfer.

The concept of 10,000 hours of practice being necessary for true expertise has been popularized in the western world in the past couple of decades by different academics and authors, principally Malcolm Gladwell, author of *Outliers*. It is a simplification. Gladwell himself emphasizes that natural ability is also significant; the point, he says, is that: 'The amount of time to develop your abilities is probably longer than you think.'[1] There is a significant amount of academic literature supporting the conclusion that approximately ten years of apprenticeship or 10,000 hours is necessary for real mastery, although it is not always sufficient on its own. The most intensive forms of coaching and practice may be effective in trimming the amount of time necessary to practice, but the central point is that there are no significant or easy shortcuts. A study by the late University of Colorado academic Anders Ericsson in 1993 found that leading violinists had averaged considerably more hours of practice than those who did not reach the standard required to become concert violinists. His research and others have indicated that: 'Performers can acquire skills that circumvent basic limits on working memory capacity and sequential processing. Deliberate practice can also lead to anatomical changes resulting from adaptations to intense physical activity.'[2] Anders Ericsson wrote extensively about the disciplines involved in reaching expert status.[3]

Of course, 10,000 hours is both an average and an approximation. A fairly obvious point is that long hours of practice is likely to be a necessary but not a sufficient requirement for expert status. For example, individuals vary in their level of innate ability, and in their access to expert coaching. Also, some forms of practice are more valuable than others. Continual practice without good coaching can result in bad habits becoming entrenched. Some types of expertise require many hours of solo practice, whereas social skills such as leadership or counselling require more interaction. These are valid points in some contexts, but pedantic beside the bigger point, which is that dedication, persistence and commitment consistently produce better results than a half-hearted or short-term approach. The principles of long-term commitment and continual improvement are central to the discipline of total quality management, in which I have specialized for many years in my corporate career.

When I worked alongside the expert dairy farmer Glynn Durham and his equally expert manager Apan in my gap year in the early 1960s (see Chapter 11), I was working alongside two individuals who had surely exceeded their 10,000 hours. They had an intimate and innate knowledge of the herd they were attending to: to the needs of the cows and the dairy operation, and to the requirements of the customers. They had achieved a level sometimes called 'unconscious competence' – their intimate knowledge of tasks and requirements had become so deeply instilled into their practices and thoughts that their correct decisions had become akin to instinct. In the field of psychology, the concept of 'unconscious competence' is well established. Through practice, individuals can move from a state of unconscious incompetence, through conscious incompetence (beginner or learner status), to conscious competence (advanced level) and finally to unconscious competence (mastery).[4]

In the Africa Bridge approach, we emphasize the importance of identifying strengths and how exercises such as Future Search can help create this foundation of understanding. This discipline requires patience, resilience and, for many initiatives, thousands of hours of practice and improvement. Persistence, practice and determination are important – but it helps to build on existing abilities and competence. The research base also illustrates the importance of learning to correct errors and seeking to improve, covered also in Chapter 9 Continual Learning.

In the particular context of Africa Bridge, the inherent strengths in the communities that we were seeking to build upon were disguised by material poverty. Many individuals had clocked up several thousand hours of experience in agriculture, but often at a subsistence level owing to lack of investment. High-yielding crops or dairy farms require specialist equipment and resources such as fertilizers. Similarly, entrepreneurial flair is hard to teach, and though it was present within the villages, it represented another strength that was thwarted by lack of investment capital and inadequate infrastructure. The latent talent, therefore, was considerable, and it made sense to develop these, rather than begin projects for which there would be little or no prior experience and expertise.

The core strengths in the rural communities discussed in the previous chapter that Africa Bridge sought to build upon were:

1. Agricultural tradition and expertise.
2. Entrepreneurial ability, including multiple skills and resourcefulness.
3. High respect for education.
4. Community cohesion and caring for vulnerable children.

In addition, we as founders of Africa Bridge had certain inherent strengths and accumulated knowledge. As principal founder, I had

some experience of agriculture and dairy farming (see Chapter 11
Early Years) and significantly more experience in managerial
processes, including total quality and Future Search. Other individuals on the board of Africa Bridge and among our first employees
had complementary skills. Some of the skills and experience of the
founder members of the board were: organizational development,
executive management, experience of founding a hospital in Tanzania, and psychosocial skills. In addition there was an AIDS activist,
a public relations specialist and an NGO director.

The validity of the 10,000-hour benchmark appears to have been
borne out by experience in agricultural co-operatives. When
conventional NGOs have set up agricultural co-operatives based on
a few days' training, the failure rate is nearly 100%. With the Africa
Bridge approach, in which training and development takes three
years and is allied to careful selection of members, close ties to the
community, and achieving social aims, the failure rate drops to
almost zero.

In addition to the technical learning necessary, an additional
quality that is particularly important for business enterprises, especially those in challenging circumstances, is personal and collective
resilience. This includes not just the ability to learn cognitively from
setbacks, but the emotional resourcefulness to be able to absorb
losses, recover a sense of confidence, and commit yourself to trying
again. Agriculture has many external challenges – unpredictable
weather and diseases of either crops or animals, for example. Disasters such as blight, drought or infestation are always a possibility.
Moreover, the link to socially meaningful goals, namely the work of
the Most Vulnerable Children's Committee, anchors the project
around a strong sense of purpose.

Resilience and confidence, both individual and collective, are
key attributes. The combination of applying advanced skills and
overcoming obstacles helps develop operational confidence. This is
a valuable asset that is difficult to teach, and which tends to come
through experience. Hence it was exceptionally rewarding to

observe that, when the pig farm co-operative had to be folded owing to an outbreak of swine flu, some of the participants switched quite swiftly to other enterprises that were thriving within a few months.

Some studies on how people react to setbacks seem to show that missing out on an opportunity, or incurring bad luck, can be a spur to greater application and effectiveness over the longer term. In an article in *The Times*, the author Dan Pink reported some of these findings, concluding that regret can be a positive emotion. One study looked at scientists over a 15-year period, comparing those who had just missed out on a prestigious grant with those who had been successful. Counter-intuitively, over the longer term those who had just missed out appeared to subsequently enjoy a more successful career, measured by more papers and citations. The explanation is that the regret prompted reflections of "If only...." which in turn encouraged renewed application, to seek to prevent a repeat of the disappointment. Regret, therefore, can be a positive emotion, if it prompts honest reflection and commitment to improve.[5]

In the context of aid programs or development initiatives in sub-Saharan Africa, especially when there are founders of European heritage, showing up and being persistent is important. There is a track record of promising-sounding programs folding after a short period, owing to lack of patience or commitment by donors. When I first went to Idweli to conduct the Future Search discussions prior to setting up Africa Bridge initiatives, the reception was polite and warm, but I detected an understandable skepticism that I would stay the course. It was important to keep showing up, and not to quit in response to a setback, even a major one. It was not easy in the early days. My home and family were on the other side of the ocean. There were also practical problems. The lack of infrastructure of the kind that one takes for granted in a wealthier country caused frustration: the banking system did not extend to rural areas, internet access was only available at an internet café in a city, and so on. Making payments was stressful; more than once I had to travel on a bus for 16 hours with several hundred-dollar bank notes hidden inside a waist band beneath my shirt.

One can imagine that growing up in an exceptionally deprived environment – poor quality housing, limited infrastructure and a lack of educational opportunities – leads to many feelings of 'If only....', especially if you possess ability and ambition and face formidable obstacles and incidents of bad luck. It is simplistic to say that hardship automatically generates personal resilience – too much trauma and poverty can be destructive; nonetheless, many of the individuals Africa Bridge has worked with have displayed an impressive capacity for personal growth and development, and an ability to overcome hazards and setbacks and keep on learning (see Chapter 1, Case Studies). We in the management of Africa Bridge, and on the board, have sought to at least match these individuals for perseverance and commitment to learn. We have the ambition to be a forever enterprise, at least in essence: the particular initiative may change, but the plan is that the model and its ethos will endure through several generations.

Nearly a decade in development

The Africa Bridge model took eight years to develop a pattern of services that have produced significant social and economic benefits. The first initiative was to set up an orphanage – and the first significant insight came three to four years in, upon recognizing that an orphanage was not the optimal approach (this is discussed further in Chapter 9). There then followed the idea of the agricultural co-operatives, which only began to make a major contribution to reducing child poverty when combined with the activities of the Most Vulnerable Children's Committees. We did not start this effective combination until 2008, having founded the board of Africa Bridge in 2000. The eight-year process involved a collective apprenticeship of experimentation, iterations and learning from both failures and successes. This time period is comparable to the decade or so of dedicated practice that the research indicates is necessary for the most worthwhile achievements.

The fact that I and the other Africa Bridge founders kept coming back gave us credibility. Some initiatives were more successful than others, but even with the ineffective ones, the fact that we had taken the initiative demonstrated our commitment and added to the credibility and the level of trust. Building trust is essential in order to work closely with communities. In common with developing technical ability, building trust takes time and requires patience.

KEY POINTS

- The much-cited figure of 10,000 hours of practice necessary for expertise is a simplification, but there is little doubt that dedication and commitment boost the chances of either individual or collective achievement.
- While much of the research relates to specific crafts such as learning a musical instrument, the same principles apply to human expertise more generally, including agriculture and managing organizations.
- Africa Bridge has sought to build on existing strengths, working in areas where levels of agricultural knowledge and entrepreneurial flair are high and individuals are held back through lack of resources.
- Emotional strength and personal resilience are also important factors in supporting the long-term sustainability of a project, especially given that agriculture involves significant potential external hazards, such as adverse climate and disease.
- Building trust is as important as building technical skills when committing long-term to a development project.

- The success rate for agricultural co-operatives rises dramatically from below 10% to more than 90% when accompanied by a relevant training and support program lasting years rather than a few weeks.
- The ambition of Africa Bridge is to be a forever enterprise – in terms of maintaining the ethos and providing an example/role model, although specific projects may change.

CHAPTER 8
WOMEN: A LEADING ROLE

There is a joke that often goes around social media at Christmas. It's a commentary on the Bible story, familiar to every Christian, of the Three Wise Men who arrive at the stable on the Twelfth Day to offer gifts of gold, frankincense and myrrh to the new-born baby Jesus and his family. If there had been Three Wise Women, the story goes, they would have asked for directions, arrived on time, brought practical gifts, helped deliver the baby, tidied the stable and made a nice casserole.

We smile at the story because there is an element of truth to it. In aggregate, women are more likely to notice and attend to issues within the family and the community, and care about an infant's health.

For the 10,000 years or so that humans have lived in settled communities, fed by agriculture rather than hunting and gathering, most societies have been patriarchal; at times fiercely so. There are different theories, none of them conclusive, as to why. The most intuitive relate to the time taken up by women in giving birth and raising children, freeing men to engage in politically significant roles in agriculture, industry, conquest and building cities and nations. This does not appear fully to explain the extreme prejudice against women adopting leadership roles in societies that one frequently encounters in different cultures.

We live in a world designed overwhelmingly by men. This is a problem. It has probably caused too many urban motorways and too much pollution, lack of safe spaces for women and families, displacement of communities from rural areas, and the expectation that people work and live around technology, rather than have technology serve them. The idea that the bulk of leadership roles should be arbitrarily assigned to only half the population is absurd. It is a very long-established custom – but it produces outcomes that are at best sub-optimal. It is an approach that never had an evidence base.

To correct this, we have insisted from the outset of Africa Bridge on at least 50% representation of women on every agricultural co-operative and Most Vulnerable Children's Committee (MVCC). Moreover, we have insisted on equal representation of women in leadership roles. Also, there is a proportion of at least 50% girls in the group of children who present at the Future Search meetings.

The starting point of Africa Bridge was to transform the prospects of the most vulnerable children, as a long-term project to help lift a community out of extreme poverty. Women are, on balance, more attuned to attending to the needs of children in a community. What emerges from our initial Future Search meetings, where children take the lead in discussions, is that all these children have dreams. African children are like children anywhere in the world: full of potential, full of desire to achieve, with enormous capacity to learn. I once met a girl who was malnourished; she was probably ten but looked only five, and had a distended belly. When I asked her about her aspirations, she didn't say 'Food', she said: 'I want to go to school.' Our approach is to enable the women to help the children to fulfil their dreams by enabling them to increase their incomes. It is more natural for women to want to protect and nurture their children, and other children in the community, and encourage them to fulfil their dreams. We do not feel that we have to make a business case for equal leadership roles for women. Nonetheless, there is an increasing body of literature strongly indicating that gender-balanced leadership in organizations, communities and in politics, can produce better outcomes. There are dozens of theories of leadership, thousands of research studies and millions of words devoted to the subject. Many of the theories are criticized for lacking crisp definitions and definitive proof of the efficacy of a certain approach to leadership, proven at a causal level by hard scientific evidence, compared with others. Such critiques appear valid, but perhaps they are based on an unrealizable ideal. Running an organization or being responsible for a community of diverse, sentient human beings is never going to resemble a laboratory experiment. It is more realistically understood in terms of principles and progress rather than a quest for irrefutable proof. Many of the concepts, and much of the research into organizational leadership, have some merit, and I have become acquainted with them in both my corporate career and over the past 20 years of being involved in Africa Bridge. In this book, and in the management of Africa Bridge, we take a pragmatic view: we assess whether our approach produces better outcomes – as measured by diet, health, survey questionnaire results on quality of life – than the approach we had before. We assess, as best we can, which interventions are working and do more of those; we identify those that are less effective and do less of those.

If the positive findings of all the leadership studies – at least those with a humane and liberal philosophy – could be summarized simply, they point to the importance of process, the importance of communication, and the importance of inclusion. Matters that might have previously been considered minor or soft – the way in which you talk to people, the way in which you include people, the way in which meetings are facilitated – can often be decisive to a project's success.

Much of the evidence base on leadership generally, including the dimension of gender, is North American, and much of it is corporate based. There is a natural tendency in the research to seek justification in terms of stronger commercial performance in return for this or that investment in a certain leadership approach. If the test is framed as an assessment of whether business outcomes are superior if there is a gender-balanced board, or female leadership, this reveals a certain assumption: that the case has to be made. Africa Bridge is different. Inclusion is the process as well as the goal. Involving women in leadership roles, and children in advisory roles, are givens: they are founding principles.

Our intended outcomes at Africa Bridge are both social and commercial – there isn't an inherent conflict between the two as the co-operatives have to be commercially viable to support the community, and we encourage entrepreneurship. It is also the case, based on both the evidence base and our own experience, that inclusive, participative approaches to leadership are more effective in both business and social terms.

Professor Carl Larson, an academic adviser to Africa Bridge, reports that the evidence base for effective leadership supports an approach, especially for socially focused enterprises, in which there is both a gender balance and an approach he describes as integrative, in contrast to a more calculating style categorized as distributive. This conclusion is informed by studies on negotiating styles as well as on internal leadership dynamics. There is a marked difference in a situation where an individual or group is emotionally invested in the success of a negotiation or enterprise, compared to a situation where they are just looking for the best price. An integrative style is looking for, at best, a 'win-win' or an imaginative alternative around which a consensus can be built that allows different parties to maintain their aspirations. With a distributive approach it may be a win-lose situation or, if the parties are of equal power, a trade-off.

In summary:

Integrative leadership – based on seeking an optimal outcome for the whole population – rather than a win-lose. If there are negotiations and consultation, they are likely to offer a genuine opportunity for those parties invited to influence the outcome.

Distributive leadership – based on an assumption of certain constituencies winning out over others. It is a calculating approach, reflecting the raw power different parties wield. A consultation may be token, with the major decisions already taken. A sham consultation tends to corrode trust, resulting in energy and focus becoming directed away from the project's aims.

Carl describes the characteristics of integrative leadership as bringing people together, emphasizing common goals, and being collaborative, and he confirms that Africa Bridge has adopted this approach from the beginning. The integrative approach is more likely to bring about lasting, sustainable change that harnesses the best of male and female capabilities. On balance, women display a greater tendency towards the integrative approach, although the full picture is complex. Traditional male and female strengths overlap to a significant degree – there is a distribution curve – but evidence strongly shows that integrative leadership, based on inclusive and empowering practices, are the key to sustainable social success and effective project management. A review of the handling of the Covid pandemic by different US states found that those with female governors had consistently lower rates of deaths. They were more likely to issue early stay-at-home orders, and a qualitative analysis of governor briefings concluded they were stronger on empathy.[1]

A review of the leadership literature, published in 2021, concluded: 'Promoting a richly diverse group of women into leadership roles will not only help make societal institutions, businesses and governments more representative, but can also contribute to more ethical, productive, innovative and financially successful organizations that demonstrate higher levels of collective intelligence and are less rife with conflict.'[2]

There are matters both of principle and pragmatism in the approach at Africa Bridge. It is only fair to involve the whole community, and it is more effective. The dynamics associated with the distributive, or win-lose, approach to leadership may result from male rivalry. This approach is more likely to result in sub-optimal outcomes featuring factional internal politics and a blame game. There is not a neat gender divide, however, and the personal qualities of individual leaders are decisive.

In an interview for this book, Carl Larson described more fully his findings from six decades of studying and advising on organizational cultures and styles of leadership. A key discipline of the integrative style is that the leaders keep the focus on the goal, the mission. For NASA, it may be sending someone to the moon. For Africa Bridge, it is enhancing children's prospects. This overriding sense of purpose must remain the focus. Quality of process and of collaboration are key differentiators in enhancing the prospects for successful outcomes in social enterprises, according to research. In one study in which Carl was involved, the concept of transfer of commitment emerged as the key factor.[3] He describes the features of a healthy transfer of commitment as follows:

'We have a very good understanding of that [transfer of commitment]. The effect of a high process quality is that people have a lot of confidence in it. They have a sense of empowerment by it. They're clear about how it relates to the overall collective goal. So that commitment to the overall collective effort transfers ... from the people who were bringing the program into the community, in this case, this would be a transfer from Africa Bridge to the people in the villages.'

In a healthy organization, a positive vibe is almost tangible; you can sense it as soon as you enter the workspace. People are committed, enthusiastic; they are creative and they share their ideas for improving service. They believe in what they are doing. The style of leadership and the culture in an organization or group are contagious. This is not a metaphor: moods are literally contagious at the neural level. Writing in the Harvard Business Review in 2008, as findings from social neuroscience were emerging, Daniel Goleman and Richard Boyatzis described the phenomenon as follows:

'The leader-follower dynamic is not a case of two (or more) independent brains reacting consciously or unconsciously to each other. Rather, the individual minds become, in a sense, fused into a single system.'

Mirror neurons are active in this process, resulting in moods and attitudes becoming transmitted from individual to individual, explaining the impact of a positive, healthy leadership style focused on a clear sense of purpose and good conduct.[4] These early findings have been confirmed by more recent research.[5]

Carl Larson adds: 'The leader in those healthy organizations is focused on the mission, the goal; something worthwhile. It may be fighting the pandemic, or exploring outer space. They don't allow the politics of the organization to interfere. They make decisions on the basis of the extent to which activities are helping the organization reach its goal or mission.'

The leadership style is essential for maintaining this culture – but it is also necessary to have a healthy structure or system, and well-judged incentives. Understanding how incentives work, including financial incentives, is a crucial part of setting up an enterprise. This explains the 'pass-on' principle in Africa Bridge, where a condition of membership of a co-operative is to pass on an asset to another member; however, this co-exists with the freedom to retain subsequent profits and build a business (see Chapter 3). This seeking the appropriate blend of individual motivation and community well-being has been a continual quest. We have sought a blend of an integrative, participative leadership style within a system of resource-allocation and incentives that are aimed at being fair and balanced. The problem with the orphanage, as discussed in Chapter 9 Continual Learning, was that it could not accommodate all the orphans in the area, and was therefore exclusive and inherently created a win-lose dynamic, a feature of the distributive style of leadership defined by Carl Larson and identified in the research.

• • •

Engaging the whole community

In parts of rural Tanzania, poverty is extreme. Living on $1-2 a day is pretty much impossible. Many mothers and grandmothers will take in an orphan, but every time they do so, it prejudices food security for the household, if household income is such that they are in extreme poverty. Getting out of poverty is difficult. You need everyone on the journey. It means halting the vicious spirals (low income, hard to study and invest, poor diet and health, low school attendance, preventing better careers and higher income), putting them into reverse, and patiently building the virtuous circles (better prospects for income leading to better diet, more education, more career opportunities, in turn leading to higher household income) to replace them.

In practice, membership of Africa Bridge co-operatives is nearly two-thirds women, while the proportion at MVCCs is closer to 50-50. Our experience with co-operatives is that after we linked them to an MVCC or wider community development, the success rate improved dramatically. The idea of the MVCC was originally an initiative by the Tanzanian Government initiative. But the committees did not succeed as entities on their own – the success rate was about zero. The likely explanation was that this was because they were not linked to an income generating activity. Plonked into a village, the committees weren't supported by the local economy. They were a vehicle without an engine. Setting up social and commercial entities, and linking them, has turned out to be the most effective approach. It gives you one plus one equals three, rather than an entity on its own which withers away.

Empirically we have found that creating close social and economic linkages between activities that have traditionally been seen as male – setting up businesses, asset management, financial management – and those that have been seen as female – nutrition, childcare, education, community welfare – has resulted in the best outcomes. Both genders are involved in both fields of activity, and women are encouraged and empowered to become leaders.

Our experience supports the conclusion that the effectiveness of the initiatives is attributable to involving women and the whole community, geared around the strategic objective of enhancing prospects for a community's most precious asset: the children. If they are not well educated and fed, then there is no future.

Wider empowering effect for women

The Africa Bridge model gives women a voice, often for the first time in their lives. We know from our interviews that this has contributed directly to positive agricultural, economic and social outcomes. and women's involvement – including leadership positions, not confined to supporting roles – has been integral to Africa Bridge from its early days, when we discouraged the custom of only men occupying the benches in a meeting room while women prepared the refreshments, encouraging instead equality of contributions and status. Within 18 months of these changes, women were doing much of the talking; now, often the chair of a MVCC or a co-operative is a woman.

Early on in the Africa Bridge program a priest told us: 'We tried women in leadership and it didn't work.' We didn't accept that, and we believe we have proved him wrong. Some of the most inspiring stories in Africa Bridge have been from older women, describing how they have been allowed to have their say in local politics, local businesses, and community affairs for the first time in their lives. It is transformational for their feelings of well-being, as well as for their prospects and those of their families.

An interesting side-effect of women in leadership roles has been to equip them to become successful entrepreneurs and political leaders. Women in MVCCs have to be literate, and have to be elected. They are going into schools and homes, advocating children's rights and women's rights, dealing with legal issues. They have standing in the community. This was not an explicit objective of Africa Bridge, but it is a benign and empowering side-effect that we encourage. Reola Phelps, Chair of the Board and an adviser to Africa Bridge, has observed this in the communities in which we work. She points also to the work of the philanthropist Melinda Gates, author of *The Moment of Lift*, based on the findings that empowering women tends to empower the whole community.

As Melinda Gates observed: 'Empowering women doesn't only enhance prospects for women and their families – it changes the world. If you want to lift society up, stop keeping women down. If you lift women up, you lift up humanity.'

Reola has also noted that in the wards benefiting from Africa Bridge the number of women standing for political positions has increased significantly. This is not something specifically monitored in our research, so the finding at this stage is anecdotal. But we are confident it is occurring and will encourage and monitor this promising development.

Early in the work of Africa Bridge, Reola facilitated meetings for us in Tanzania. During one early meeting she observed: 'The men were doing all of the talking and they were both complaining and demanding, but the processes we had designed were very good and led to giving everyone in the room a voice – including the women. One prominent woman, Mama Rehema, stood up. She spoke passionately of the benefits to the whole community of the work of Africa Bridge. The room became very quiet. The men were not used to hearing women speak this way. They were astounded. The other women were nodding, equally amazed by Mama Rehema speaking in this manner. The tenor of the meeting changed completely. Other women began speaking and the energy became much more positive. Later, Mama Rehema came to me and thanked me for setting up a meeting where she could speak her mind, let her voice be heard.'

Since March 2021 Tanzania has its first female president, Samia Suluhu Hassan, who immediately adopted a more pragmatic and evidence-based approach to the Covid-19 pandemic than her male predecessor. While leadership of a co-operative isn't a direct line to the presidency, it involves skills of management and advocacy.

Another adviser to Africa Bridge, Susan Stewart, who has an engineering background, observes how taking a leading role in agricultural co-operatives has dramatically increased the influence of women, not least because the enterprises are the mainstay of the rural economy. 'They had gone from having no voice to being leaders in the village.' She observes a direct link between this leadership role and the significant improvements in diet, health, housing, and prospects that have followed the setting up of an Africa Bridge program in a ward.

KEY POINTS

- Involving women in leadership roles is a key founding principle for Africa Bridge. There is a rule that membership of an MVCC and co-operative has to be at least 50% female; similarly, the proportion of children involved in Future Search must be at least 50% girls.
- While it has not been necessary to make a 'business case' for female leadership, nonetheless research does show that an approach to leadership that can be regarded as integrative, combined with gender-balance in leadership teams, can lead to better outcomes, both socially and economically.
- Getting out of extreme poverty is difficult. It helps to harness the skills of the whole community.
- A benign side effect of Africa Bridge has been an enhanced role in the community, and in politics, by women.

CHAPTER 9
CONTINUAL LEARNING

To understand the currents in the water,
He who wishes to know the truth, must enter the water.
Nisargadatta

No battle plan survives first contact with the enemy, according to established military wisdom. Or, as the British artist Bridget Riley observed, quoting the French artist Matisse: 'Don't get rid of your mistakes.' She adds: 'They are the things that will help you to get to move, and to think, and to understand a little bit more about what you're doing.'[1] In life, in business, as in art, you are more likely to succeed if you learn from your mistakes, learn from experience generally, and learn the right lessons. Generally, in social programs and in business, the most effective organizations are continually iterating, learning, absorbing lessons and adapting to a relentlessly changing world.

The original working title for this chapter was 'Learn from Your Mistakes'. This is a healthy discipline, but it is too narrow a focus. What we've learned in Africa Bridge, building on the more enlightened management principles I absorbed earlier in my career, is to learn from everything. Learn every day. Learn from what works, as well as what doesn't.

The categorization of a course of action as being a 'mistake' or a success is sometimes too binary in its conception; many initiatives in complex situations have both positive and negative consequences. A course of action may have some merit but turn out to be sub-optimal and can be improved with reform. Also, there's a category of decisions that are perfectly logical and sound on the basis of the information available, but external events (political change, bad weather) mean that the project becomes unviable. For example, at Africa Bridge in the 2000s we set up a pig farm co-operative that was initially highly promising – but there was an outbreak of swine flu a couple of years later, and the pigs had to be slaughtered and the enterprise shut down.

Perhaps the Tanzanian government's failure to make a success with Most Vulnerable Childrens' Committees is an example of a situation where the government did not appreciate the complexity of starting and sustaining MVCCs. Yet when started in a different context, with different partnerships and style of leadership, we made them successful institutions.

One of my earliest ideas after starting in Africa Bridge had nothing to do with agriculture. I had an entrepreneurial idea in the realm of health. After taking early retirement and moving back to Tanzania in the early 2000s, I was initially based in Tanga on the north coast of Tanzania. It is a part of the country of which I had fond memories, because my family had been based there when I was a young child. We had an idyllic lifestyle with a home on the beach and swimming in the dazzling coral reefs. I learned upon my return that there was only one western-trained doctor for every 33,000 patients; also, that many people consulted with traditional healers, in some cases using herbal-based treatments. One of these had passed a test by the World Health Organization as being effective for patients with early to mid-stage AIDS. It had been developed by Bongo

Mzizi. At the time, western medicines were out of reach for most Tanzanian citizens, so a diagnosis was a death sentence. My idea was to form a collaboration between western-trained doctors and herbalists; the former have access to western medicines, the latter are the link to the patients. I floated this idea to the Tanga regional medical officer, who thought the idea had much potential. Despite his support for the idea, it never took hold. He told me that there was too much resistance from the western-trained doctors, who would not collaborate with the herbalists. This opposition struck me as being unimaginative and limiting, given that western medicines were simply not an option for so many, and the proposed tie-up held the potential to enhance the reach of both traditional and modern treatments, with the overall effect of reducing suffering. It was shortly after this episode that Dr Neema Mgana, a United Nations adviser, invited me to Idweli, the southwest region of Rungwe on the other side of the country, to carry out a needs analysis to help the orphans there. As described in Chapter 3, this ultimately led to the first agricultural co-operatives being established – but not before we had tried another venture that was to have a relatively short life.

Is an orphanage the solution for a high rate of orphans?

After our initial Future Search meetings in Idweli, everything seemed to point to an orphanage as the solution to meet the most immediate social need that was presenting – which was a locally high number of orphans. This was mostly caused by AIDS but made worse by the tragic death of more than 40 adults as a result of a petrol tanker fire in 2001. Neema was involved with Godfrey's Children charity, set up in memory of her fiancé. Another partner was the Lundy Foundation, whose founder funded a study into the needs of vulnerable children.

This combination seemed to support the idea of helping orphaned children directly. Also contributing to the decision was our consultation with some local children as part of the Future

Search process. This included some who were too young to be involved in full discussions, and whom we invited to participate by painting pictures. Many of them drew pictures of buildings that, to some of the other western advisers and me, resembled an orphanage. So the message seemed clear.

As an institution, the orphanage we built in Idweli was not obviously a mistake in the short-term, literal sense of the world. It housed, fed and helped educate many children. But there were two problems that would not go away: it was exclusive and it was not sustainable. The high rate of orphans meant that we did not have the resources to accommodate all those in need – only around 50 out of the 300 locally. The children who had been admitted thrived: they had access to three meals a day, good housing, and lighting for evening study, contributing to improved academic outcomes . But by its exclusive nature, it was divisive and caused resentment among those not admitted. Secondly, we failed to establish a way to ensure it was sustainable economically. In practice, it needed annual donations from the Africa Bridge charity to keep it going. This was not the regenerative, economically sustainable enterprise that we had originally envisaged.

Moreover, the problem that the orphans faced, once analyzed and understood in more depth, was not so much a lack of a roof over a child's head, but lack of other resources. This was not a city – these were villages with a strong sense of community. In practice, in the villages an orphan would be taken in, but this kind act would stretch the limited resources of a household even further. The focus for us became improving the economic prospects of a wider range of households and children, lifting the villages as a whole out of poverty. Unless you solve poverty you're never going to stop paying into a non-income-generating project.

First of all, the sensitive and difficult operation of closing the orphanage would have to be managed. The closure was phased over a period of several months, and Africa Bridge directly supported the families taking the children back in with financial support for a year.

The co-operatives, meanwhile, were being set up before the closure of the orphanage, and every effort was made to ensure that the families taking children in would have every opportunity to take part in the new enterprises – and in practice, many did.

The idea for setting up co-operatives was influenced in part by a serendipitous meeting I had with Lutheran and Moravian churches running charitable enterprises in the country. While Catholic organizations focused on uniforms and books for the children, these churches were piloting co-ops. The Moravian church was working in partnership with the sustainable agriculture charity Heifer International. The idea of co-operatives suggested itself as a regenerative, profitable vehicle for improving the prospects of the community – including the most vulnerable children. Moreover, I had some background and knowledge of farming, as I had accompanied my father on work trips in his role as an agricultural adviser and had worked in agriculture for a year as a young man before switching degree subjects. So while I was no expert, my tacit knowledge and technical knowledge were not negligible.

When we experimented with pig and potato co-ops in Idweli, both were highly successful. The ward councillor, the most significant local politician, who had supported the closure of the orphanage, said to me of the co-ops: 'This is the route we have to take.'

The learning organization

There is a considerable amount of academic literature on the concept of the learning organization: the idea that a human enterprise should be continually seeking, experimenting, iterating, learning and improving. My career had included significant roles in business operations, training and development, and total quality management which, when implemented properly, instils the practices of working back from the customer's needs, working in close partnership with colleagues, and seeking continual improvement to processes and to service. This had been my specialism at a corporate role in Abbott Laboratories in the 1990s, after I had relocated from Germany to Chicago in 1989. The President of the Diagnostics Division appointed me and a Total Quality Management practitioner to introduce total quality throughout the division. I was given sufficient autonomy to do so comprehensively, and it was one of the most rewarding posts I have ever held – working with different customers, departments and cultures globally in order to improve quality and service continually. By the end of the decade, I was appointed Director of Learning and Development.

Africa Bridge is a small organization and this has helped us to maintain the practices of agility and continual learning. There is little to no bureaucracy. We have been able to learn as we go, adapt as we learn. We have tried to ensure that each venture is more effective than the last; if it isn't, we to try to understand why. This has meant imaginative thinking and exploring forms of collaboration, as well as specific initiatives.

The co-operatives were more effective than the orphanage, but initially membership wasn't sufficiently geared to those most in need. This caused resentment and loss of resources, so we needed to take greater care in identifying candidates for co-op membership. The Most Vulnerable Children's Committees (MVCCs) also offered much potential, and again we learned to take progressively more rigor and care in selecting individuals in need of help. We had a method of identifying the most vulnerable children, but this rested much responsibility and judgement on the shoulders of a small number of people. Would there be a way of being more participative, without it becoming unmanageable? Our aim was fairness: who would be the judge? We gradually expanded the number of people involved in the selection of most vulnerable children and their households, and the democratic checks and balances underpinning the process (see Chapter 3). We learned of the idea of combining the co-operatives and the MVCCs, to ensure the social enterprises were supported by the local economy and generative enterprises, rather than being reliant on donations – but how to go about this? We had to learn as we went. With every initiative, we sought to be aware of its potential and its limitations.

The text box (*see end of chapter*) shows an initial approach by Africa Bridge, alongside a superior approach that we adopted in the light of experience and evidence. It can be seen that the initiatives in the left-hand column were hardly 'mistakes'; rather, they were initiatives that led to some social benefits, but the outcomes were sub-optimal when compared with our aspirations for the community. All healthy organizations grow and develop by learning. This is true in the commercial sector as well as the voluntary sector. If we stop learning, the culture stagnates and there is a risk the enterprise will die.

Local leadership and the importance of listening

There is a need for great sensitivity on the part of westerners involved in aid or economic development programs in Africa, because of colonial history and the continuing regional inequalities of income. Those of us with a western background have to be wary of assuming we have greater knowledge or expertise than the people in the regions in which we're working, and at Africa Bridge we have always sought to work in partnership. Owing to my background in the corporate world, I do have access to potential investors and donors, as well as a background in management and organizational development.

The disciplines of the 'learning organization', when implemented conscientiously, encourage working in partnership. And one of the most important of these is something that is rarely highlighted in management development and training – listening. Managers are often coached on how to communicate; more rarely on how to listen. Abbott Laboratories, my former employer, was a corporate donor to Africa Bridge, and it was one of the company's Tanzanian employees, Alfred Magalla, who suggested to me the idea of the MVCCs and linking them to the co-operatives. So, while the major leaps forward in learning in the 20 years of Africa Bridge – the co-ops, the MVCCs and the close co-operation between the two – are consistent with corporate literature on the learning organization in which I have been trained, the actual innovations stem from ideas by Tanzanians. The model is an African innovation. I have encouraged it, but I cannot claim credit for its invention. Where I give myself credit is in having had the humility to listen.

In western business practices, and in much discussion on economics and policies at a political level, a weakness has been to segregate social and profit-making activities – in some cases to an excessive degree. A business's 'corporate social responsibility' initiatives are often completely separate from its money-making activities. At a policy level, economic development is considered separately from social care policies. Some distinction between the respective activities is necessary, but if this is taken too far there is a risk that the mutual dependencies are underestimated or misunderstood completely. Social endeavors ultimately rely upon a thriving local economy; similarly, businesses depend upon an effective social sector to provide healthcare, education, and a strong community with low crime. At Africa Bridge, we feel we have demonstrated this interdependency at a micro level, with the effective coordination of the MVCCs and the agricultural businesses. This will be a feature of all societies.

Issue	Initial Approach	Revised Approach
Clients	Orphans	Most Vulnerable Children
Orphan care	Orphanage	Increase Family incomes thru Co-ops
Co-ops sustainability	Improve co-op process	Combine Co-ops with MVCC
Choice of co-op Participants	Defined by school teachers	Defined by data from MVCC census
Determinant of Co-op entrants	Driven by family vulnerability	Driven by family vulnerability + readiness
Co-op's ability to survive threats	Little preparation	Well prepared. E.g., vaccine supply chains established

SUMMARY

At Africa Bridge, we made many missteps in the early years, but the learning was instructive. The most effective leaders, and communities or organizations, display grit or resilience. They do not stop striving or learning amid difficulties or even apparently catastrophic events. They display individual and collective resilience. Many entrepreneurs become successful not with their original idea for a business, but a significantly different business offering that resulted from their change and adaptation in the light of first contact with the market – and second contact, and third, and so on. Progress in any real human enterprise is bumpy. Not all the co-operatives we have set up have thrived, particularly the early ones, though the vast majority have. Some have been affected by disasters such as swine flu or unpredictable weather. The concept of the learning organization, while a good one, can sometimes be misunderstood as aspiring to a situation where progress is smooth and continuous. This doesn't happen in real life! As with switching from the orphanage to a different strategy, it was a good decision, but involved some loss and disruption. Emotional ownership and engagement in an enterprise is often encouraged by leadership textbooks. It is a tremendous asset to nurture, since if people feel convinced of the necessity and identify with the purpose of an enterprise it helps to unleash reserves of commitment; but it can also make it difficult to disengage from a project amid clear evidence that it is not working, or is not the best option. The learning organization can involve loss and emotional pain, as well as progress and a feeling of fulfilment. But continual learning is essential for continued relevance, growth and prosperity.

KEY POINTS

- Learn from your mistakes – but also from initiatives that work out well. It helps to treat every day as a learning opportunity.
- Entrepreneurs often switch the type of service they offer in response to reactions from customers and learning from the effectiveness of different approaches.
- The first Africa Bridge initiatives were respectively a medical initiative and an orphanage, before we settled on agricultural co-operatives and later the MVCCs.
- A corporate background in total quality and the learning organization have been applied to Africa Bridge.
- Learning, and change, often involve loss as well as growth and can be emotionally painful.
- A most underrated quality in leadership is listening – the breakthrough innovations in Africa Bridge have come from Tanzanians with local knowledge.
- Tenacity and resilience are essential qualities for enterprises to succeed in a sustainable way.

CHAPTER 10
LOVE IS A VERB
THE IMPORTANCE OF PASSION AND PURPOSE

African Parable
A woman is sitting beside the road in need of help
A man approaches her, wanting to help
She says to him:
'If you are here to help me
You are wasting your time
If you are here for your own liberation
You may help me.'

first met the business executive Bill O'Brien in 1997 in the Catskill Mountains at the Mohonk Mountain House about 90 miles north of New York, at a conference that was part of the Synchronicity movement (see Chapter 12 Early Years 2). Bill sat on the stage in his jacket and tie, stern-faced, looking every inch the hard-nosed corporate man. Yet when the interviewer asked him how he had turned around a failing bank, he replied in a gruff voice: 'With love'.

These were not the words I was expecting to hear. Expanding upon the theme, he defined love as an active verb, not something you get but something you give. It means 'to complete another'. For a leader, your actions are to help your employees and customers enhance their quality of life and reach their goals. The binding passion that lends purpose to Africa Bridge is love: a desire to improve the prospects of vulnerable children in a sustainable way.

It is after some hesitation, and following reflection and discussion with others, that I decided to use the 'L' word in a book on economic and social development and empowerment. The word 'love' comes with multiple meanings, and each individual's experience of its use is probably unique. A careless use of the term may encourage extravagant but wasteful initiatives based more upon the heart than the head. And then there are the romantic connotations, which leads individuals down a very different path of thought altogether …

There is a limitation with the English language, as a single word covers many meanings. The ancient Greeks developed four words for love: eros (romantic, sexual love), storge (family love) philia (the bonding with someone of similar beliefs), and agape (altruism, empathy and a love of humanity). Bill's philosophy, and the binding ethos of Africa Bridge, is best described in this lexicon as *agape*. In addition, however, his definition of love being the completion of another enhances the potential for experiencing all four meanings of love.

In business, ethical and commercial goals are often described as distinct or in inherent opposition, which is unhelpful and inaccurate. It is possible, though not easy, to please both head and heart; but more fundamentally, a humanitarian objective is of little use if the organization is financially a failure. I agree with Martin Luther King when he said: 'Power without love is reckless and abusive. Love without power is sentimental and anemic.'

In an interview for this book, businessman and friend to Africa Bridge Carl Sardegna challenges the arbitrary divide, which is common in western economic thinking, between seeking to be profitable and seeking to be ethical and practise *agape*. There can be prejudices on both sides: those focused on commercial goals may see compassion and love as a soft-hearted distraction, while many in the humanitarian sector develop a suspicion of for-profit enterprises, despite their economic necessity if an enterprise, community or local economy is to be sustainable. Carl says:

'Many people who are involved in NGOs and humanitarian endeavors are doing it out of their heart and their soul and then somehow, somewhere in their history, somewhere in the development of society, they consider that it is impossible for an organization to be for profit and have the same motivations that they have.'

Financial viability is essential for sustainability, he points out. Carl's insight is counter-intuitive to some; he observes that being commercially viable, provided you do so in a responsible way, is helpful to humanitarian objectives. He says Africa Bridge has found the right balance between head and heart by setting up for-profit enterprises within a wider co-operative and setting the goal as enhancing the prospects of the most vulnerable children. Enabling entrepreneurs to retain much of their profit for themselves and for reinvestment, while sharing some of the rewards with the community, helps ensure sustainability and growth, and the opportunities for intergenerational transfer. He also points to the detail that we write binding contracts, including the requirement to give to the Most Vulnerable Children's Committees, which he says helps to institutionalize the approach of mutual benefits.

The focus on helping the community's children is a binding cause, one that no one can reasonably oppose. It is beneficial in multiple ways, boosting social and economic prospects for the community's future in addition to meeting an immediate humanitarian need.

I would observe the overwhelming similarities between for-profit and non-profit organizations: both have customers, and it is in their interests to treat their customers well – for NGOs, these are our clients, the end users of the services Africa Bridge sets up. Both have investors – for NGOs, investors are the donors, who want to see a return – this is measured in social and humanitarian terms, rather than financially, but NGOs do expect to see a return. Both types of organization need to make a surplus to be sustainable. Both benefit from a strong sense of purpose. Both need policies and procedures and a board of governance. The biggest difference in my case was that when I travelled for Abbott I sat in the front of the aircraft, and when I travel for Africa Bridge I sit at the back and pay for my fare.

Purpose generates resilience

Love, or more precisely *agape*, creates a strong sense of purpose, which in turn generates resilience. If you have a group of people pursuing a humanitarian objective that is demonstrating that it can improve people's lives, then the collective will to persist in achieving that objective is extremely strong. It may dip at times, but commitment remains high. This is a tremendous asset – arguably the most powerful one that any human enterprise can possess, so generating and nurturing this collective engagement ought to be a priority, especially in the field of social and economic development.

Without this sense of love/*agape* – otherwise expressed as a sense of purpose and passion – I would have given up Africa Bridge. We were threatened directly, early on in the enterprise. It felt like a battle for the organization's survival, because that is exactly what it was. It could even have become a battle for our actual survival. In the first ward in which we operated, Isongole, we set up an orphanage. Many of us began to realize that its establishment had become divisive, as it offered significant advantages to some children, but owing to the demand this meant excluding many more.

As described in Chapter 9, we began the delicate negotiation of running down numbers at the orphanage, obviously without making any children homeless, and reorienting our efforts towards initiatives that were self-sustaining. This drew opposition, however. It emerged that individuals from one family had begun nurturing ambitions around creating a for-profit school, beginning with our small institution. It became clear that our strategic reset, seeking to establish co-operatives and help the whole community of vulnerable children, clashed with these individuals' ambitions. It started to become quite ugly. I and other leading members of Africa Bridge, including our staff member Martha, were subjected to threats. We were beginning to experience the 'H' word, the opposite of love. We asked the District Commissioner to step in. She carried out an investigation into the family members, and the chief of police carried out his own investigation. The Commissioner called the family members in for a meeting, which was also attending by the Chief Justice, the chief of police, the chief of the army, the chief of prisons, and the district lawyer. She told the family: 'If there is any more of this behavior to Barry Childs or the staff of Africa Bridge, or any issue, you see these gentlemen in this room? You will be seeing them. Goodbye.'

The harassment stopped. Another key individual was the Ward Councillor Armon Mwalupindi, who backed our change to the co-operatives and helped enormously in the transition. Armon always talked about me in the context of the love I give to the Tanzanian people. Love is not a word one hears often from politicians in Europe or North America.

At all the most difficult times, when we faced not mere obstacles but serious threats generating real fear, the driving force that kept us moving forward was the commitment to the vulnerable children – the humanitarian mission. It was the collective love/*agape* that ensured continued momentum and progress. A strategy without this passion or commitment lacks energy.

Clearly the relative pragmatism and liberalism of Tanzanian politics helped, together with the strong sense of hospitality. The moral courage and principle of the District Commissioner, the Chief of Police and the Ward Councillor, their similar ethos and capability for *agape*, were crucial in enabling us to continue our ventures. In a corrupt or authoritarian regime our project would probably have ended at this point, but love managed to find a way to continue.

. . .

Purpose and love can boost performance

The concept of integrative leadership – seeking an optimal outcome for the whole community, rather than a confrontational win-lose dynamic – is discussed in Chapter 2 Different Ways of Thinking, and in Chapter 8 Women Take a Leading Role, which references the research of Carl Larson, an academic adviser to Africa Bridge, and others. There is a related evidence base showing strongly that a sense of purpose and passion unleashes higher performance in teams, across different sectors and types of organization. An article in the *Harvard Business Review* in 2019 reported that:

'Purpose is a grand word, but in the end, it's about helping people see their impact on others and helping them develop a story about why they love what they do. If you keep that in mind, and take a personal, authentic, and perpetual approach, you're likely to find success.'[1]

Another evidence base is the work of Professor Vlatka Hlupic, who explicitly refers to the importance of passion as well as purpose in identifying the behavioral dynamics of highly effective organizations. Her research has resulted in the concept of five 'levels' of engagement and performance, from Level 1 – characterized by low morale, conflicting internal ambitions and other dysfunctions; to Level 5 – the highest levels of coordinated productive activity empowered by passion and a strong sense of purpose. She challenges the idea that exploitation is the route to highest profits, and profiles multiple cases of organizations which combine fulfilling careers, ethical principles and strong performance indicators. In both the for-profit and non-profit sectors she identifies broadly comparable dynamics. She says: 'Work should be enlivening, enriching, sustaining; a place where we can thrive and combine work and life together.'[2]

. . .

Completing the personal circle

For me, going back to Tanzania at the start of my early retirement from corporate life gave me a sense of circularity, as it was in Tanzania that I enjoyed a happy and carefree childhood, much of it in the wonderful outdoors. When I returned to the country in 1998, I wondered what had happened to the Tanzanian children I had played with in the 1950s. Probably, I reflected somberly, many of them had died. By contrast, as a white privileged individual, I was still in good health in my middle years. This was a truly shocking contrast: life expectancy in Tanzania only surpassed 50, a full three decades less than in wealthy countries, in the 2000s. This realization was reason enough to begin an initiative such as Africa Bridge. My former friends had probably remained in the village in which they were born their whole lives, and experienced struggle and hardship. Was there a possibility of preventing such hardship and limited prospects for the current generation of Tanzanian children, or at least a proportion of the population?

The haunting memory of a young boy begging on the dockside in Egypt, nearly half a century earlier, and my feelings of privilege, impotence, and vague spiritual malaise, still lingered. Throughout the 1990s, this very personal yearning to resolve a sense of spiritual incompleteness had been growing. The decision to commit to humanitarian initiatives towards the end of the decade was not sudden, but rather the culmination of several years of reflection, during a period when personal fulfillment in my career had faded. I had begun keeping a journal, writing poems, meditating, attending meetings in the Synchronicity movement, all of which represented a growing sense that while material success in terms of career, home and personal savings had been personally rewarding up to a point, something was missing. My achievements had been built partly upon a foundation of privilege. It was my duty to try to extend similar opportunities to those who had not been fortunate enough to receive such privilege, purely through accident of birth. So, when the African-American delegates at the Chicago conference (see

Chapter 12 Early Years 2) commented that they liked it best when I talked about Africa, this was the tipping point to a major personal decision. I had a retirement fund and could have engaged in leisure activities for the rest of my life, but I decided to make a difference instead.

The concept of love – all dimensions: *agape, philia, storge* and *eros* – was increasingly at the heart of my personal life during this period. My understanding of it incorporates the sense of becoming more complete as a person. I have found this to be relevant and empowering for all aspects of my life: marriage, family, friendships, work, and spirituality. My background in a colonial family, being privileged among people who are struggling, was a form of incompleteness. You are lacking in the true love of reciprocity and mutuality that can only be found in a healthy, co-operative community. Having inherited privilege is considerably more comfortable than being non-privileged, but it is not a spiritually healthy place. Wanting to correct this involves more emotions than just guilt; it is closer to a quest to end a hollowness inside, a sense of incompleteness.

As with bringing the word 'Love' into a book about social and economic development, one has to take care when discussing a personal sense of completeness and spiritual direction. It can sound rather Californian and 'woo-woo'. And I suppose, if one's actions are limited to going on retreats and thinking about things in a certain way, there could be a tendency towards narcissism. This is similar to Martin Luther King's point about love without power being at the risk of becoming sentimental and without purpose. The point for Africa Bridge is to ally a personal sense of direction with a wider sense of humanitarian purpose. Seeking to become 'spiritual' and identifying a sense of self without this wider purpose is somewhat self-indulgent. On the other hand, being practical without a humanitarian purpose allied to a personal sense of fulfilment risks building institutions as an end in itself, constructing organizational empires at risk of corruption or just a general loss of direction.

The sense of completeness, of being both practical and spiritual, can be used to guide all activities, including in the intellectual sphere. We seek completeness in the academic studies into the findings of Africa Bridge when we not only collate data on the material outcomes, but also qualitative insights into the personal ambitions and drives, and the changes in quality of life.

SUMMARY

I am not an intellectual, but I would argue that both the Africa Bridge project, and this book, are the result of much deep reflection and thought, as well as action. It has been immensely rewarding to see the results validated by independent academic study, and to see my thoughts are similar to those of some of the thinkers quoted in this book, as I have sought to combine a search for personal sense of direction and purpose.

There is much wisdom in the African parable at the beginning of this chapter; that the most sustainable and beneficial forms of humanitarian activity are based on *agape*, and are mutual, rather than a more unequal giver-and-receiver transaction. So if someone says to me that a principal driver for me in setting up Africa Bridge is personal development and fulfilment for myself, I would reply: 'Yes, you are probably right. And your point is...?'

PART FOUR

HOW AFRICA BRIDGE CAME ABOUT

CHAPTER 11
EARLY YEARS – 1
A PERSONAL JOURNEY

'**N**o mother, no father, no curry, no rice.'

The small boy, dressed in a ragged shirt and shorts, hunger and desperation in his eyes, looks at me as he begs. He is pleading, his arms outstretched. It is 1950, and we are on the dockside in Port Said, the northern end of the Suez Canal. The heat is stifling, and the air is ripe with the smell of decaying fruit. My family and I are en route to Britain from our home in Tanzania, then called Tanganyika. I am six years old, about the same age as the boy begging before me. Age is our only common point. I am well fed, educated, travelling in comfort. I want to help, but feel helpless. I turn to my father, tears welling in my eyes. He hands me a coin. I hand it to the grateful boy who walks away. It does not seem enough.

The boy's words haunted me for years afterwards; indeed, for decades, along with the impulse of wanting to do more than offer a coin. It would be 50 years before I would begin to act upon this vague ambition.

I was born into a world that no longer exists; into a white British colonial family at a time when the UK governed around one quarter of the territory of the world, and it was still widely accepted that people of European descent were entitled to rule over large parts of Africa, Asia, the Caribbean and the Pacific region. My father's responsibilities as a specialist agricultural adviser within this regime were comparatively benign. I would accompany him on farm visits and I loved to be driven around in our trusty World War II army jeep, which my Dad loved so much he had the engine reconditioned three times. By the end of its life it had completed over 300,000 miles. I loved it also, and he had a toy replica made for me to drive in; I would hurtle down steep banks, fortunately never coming to harm.

My father's work was mostly advice to arable farmers. He helped Tanzanian farmers improve yields from their crops, and British settlers find crops that they could grow profitably. I recall fields of maize and potatoes. There were some orchards for citrus fruits and, near the coast, coconuts. I loved accompanying my Dad. While my early introduction to agricultural methods fell short of a formal apprenticeship in arable farming, through overheard conversations I would learn about the best times to sow, the risk of pests and disease, the times to harvest, and the natural rhythms of Tanzania's tropical climatic regions.

In truth, my childhood was idyllic. For a period, we lived in a pleasant home near the Indian Ocean in the northern Tanzania port town of Tanga. My parents developed a love of snorkelling, and we would swim and view the dazzling coral reefs and tropical fish. My mother can best be described as a water baby, happiest running along the beach, her hair flowing behind her, or face down in the ocean with her mask, snorkel and flippers, exploring the sensational coral reefs and dazzling fish, or walking along the low tide mark searching for rare shells. We lived in a house on a point that formed the mouth of Tanga harbor. The ocean was to the east and the harbour to the west. My parent's bedroom faced the ocean, while the sitting and dining room faced the harbour.

I retain vivid memories of some of the colonial characters from this vanished world; there was the couple George and Elsie Nestle, with whom I stayed from time to time when my parents were on a business trip to Dar es Salaam. George, a large man, was a big game hunter. He taught me where to swim in the river, with one of his rangers keeping guard with a rifle should any crocodile get too close. Colonel William Scupham would drink an evening beer and smoke a cigar sat on the veranda of the local bar. He never smoked a cigarette: 'The paper will poison you, young lad,' he informed me – advice that I took to heart and for which I remain grateful. I would call him Billy Scumbum. He approved, as he poured me a beer for my under-age palate. There was the pasty-faced administrator with a reputation for inappropriate behaviour with young women, who acquired a corresponding nickname. In my outspoken, ingenuous manner, I addressed him with his earned soubriquet at a social gathering: 'So you're the amorous tapeworm?' I asked, prompting much merriment all round.

My parents' comparatively liberal, certainly laissez-faire, attitude meant that they were relaxed about me playing with the local Tanzanian children. For me, equality was as natural as breathing. I was aware that our family had more resources than the African children with whom I would play games, but I did not consider that this conferred any social superiority. As I grew up, I discovered there was a subtly different view of life among my parents' generation, observing a rather nuanced attitude. My mother and father genuinely loved the Tanzanians they knew and worked with, yet they would not invite any as house guests. Overhearing the older generation in the European clubs, one would come across somewhat condescending attitudes, yet there was no doubt that my father genuinely desired to improve living standards and prospects for the people he advised.

The British establishment seemed to harbour similar inconsistency, an attitude often described as hypocrisy; yet perhaps it was something closer to a form of confusion, a sense of considering themselves sort-of equal with the people they governed, yet not equal, a democracy yet also an empire. The reason my family were travelling back to Britain, making a stop at Port Said and elsewhere, was to spend six months in Britain. It was policy that colonial administrators should be required to do this every three years, to prevent us from 'going native'. With my father, the policy backfired completely. He hated living in England and the policy caused him to love Africa all the more.

Given such a confused mix of contradictions and inconsistencies in British policy, it was hardly surprising that the system was becoming unstable. Within less than a generation of our stop-over in Port Said, the British Empire was all but over, with nations such as Tanzania gaining independence.

As a young man I had a rebellious streak. The relative freedom of a childhood spent mostly in the great outdoors, my instinctive attitude to racial equality from my youngest age, socializing with African kids, meant that I was destined for some bruising encounters, because as a teenager and young man I studied at high school and university in the apartheid South Africa of the 1960s. This was one of the harshest and most inhumane regimes in modern history. It was a state of institutionalized violence. Even the white boys such as myself were frequently caned. Treatment of black South Africans constituted a crime against humanity. I was shocked that people of African descent were restricted to junior, subservient roles, and that I was not expected to form a relationship of equals with them.

At my boarding school I was caned numerous times. Yet I escaped punishment for the most daring escapade, which involved a dawn escape from the dormitory by shinning down a drainpipe and helping my friend try to steal honey from an apiary. In the process, I managed to lose my shoes, and ended up with thorns in my foot. For the benefit of the school matron, as she tended to my wounded foot, I invented a tale to do with losing my boots at rugby practice. She simply raised an eyebrow and said: 'Really?'

My rebellious instinct was in part inherited: I recall my father displayed what I regarded as a healthy disrespect for his superiors in the British colonial service. Once, in South Africa, when ordered off a 'blacks only' bus, he refused to disembark, telling the policeman: 'I travel on whatever bus I like'. My father and I were both inclined to be of strong opinions, and we clashed on my choice of career. Inspired by my field trips with him in the jeep as agricultural adviser when still a boy, I announced that I wanted to be a farmer. He refused to support me financially in this ambition, advising me that it was a poor career choice. We settled on a compromise: I would take a gap year, and work on a farm for the experience.

I attended a large agricultural show and inquired about applying for a job with the country's best farmers. Two of them turned me down, but Glynn Durham, an experienced dairy farmer, took me on. He had a considerable amount of land and properties. I discovered that one of my unofficial duties was to help care for his ageing mother, as I was lodged with her. My official job title was Dairy Manager. This was an embarrassment because there was already a highly capable de facto manager in post. Apan was a native African, and under the absurd segregationist rules was not permitted to hold a managerial post. He was the real expert, and the two of us conspired in a delicate dance to maintain the outward fiction that I was his manager while, in practice, I deferred to and learned from him. Apan loved the cows. Each of the 80 cows had a name, which they responded to. The dairy could only take 45 cows at a time for milking, so the cows were split into two shifts. Each cow knew which shift it was on and which stall it was to go to. Apan knew exactly how much feed and concentrates to give to each cow. The diet varied constantly depending on the cow herself and where she was in lactation. Apan knew how all this worked, he taught me how to inoculate the cows against various diseases, how to treat mastitis of the udder and methods of hygiene. He never allowed me to make a mistake concerning those cows. And he did it all with humility, love and good grace.

The apartheid system would almost be grotesquely comic had it not been so cruel, and thousands of sane and humane people conspired to subvert its intentions. As an aside, I would observe how admirable it is that so many Africans have been capable of forgiveness and restraint. Apan never showed resentment at the discrimination he endured. At a national level, Nelson Mandela and Archbishop Desmond Tutu organized the peace and reconciliation process, which enabled white officials and police officers to escape prison for the most brutal violent offences committed under the regime if they met with their victims and showed genuine remorse. I have not come across Europeans capable of such grace and capacity for forgiveness. In a remarkable quote, Mandela once observed that he gave dignity to the white man, as there is no dignity in being an oppressor, an observation reflecting profound moral genius. In another quote, he produced what is effectively the operating motto of Africa Bridge:

'Like slavery and apartheid, poverty is not natural. It is man-made and it can be overcome and eradicated by the actions of human beings.'

Dairy farming on a large farm is hard work, I discovered. An unexpected benefit was that I had a tough work-out every day, and my physique improved. Subsequently this was to help me on the rugby field at university. While I learned much operational detail about how to run a dairy farm during my year's work experience, I also learned the sobering economic reality of setting oneself up as a young individual in an industry that was capital-intensive with low margins. You needed to be of a certain scale, and have both investment and low debt. In effect, to become a farmer you had to inherit either land or a small fortune. Reluctantly, I had to acknowledge that my father was right. Although I still wanted a career in the wide-open spaces, I opted to read geography and psychology, other subjects that interested me and which could open up opportunities for a professional career, at the University of Natal.

I studied at university, but I was not the model student. Along with other students we set up a social club called the Dodo Club, which held late-night parties and became popular. We parodied the apartheid regime at one drunken fancy dress parade. We were irrev-erent – not overtly political, but we were on the edge of acceptable behaviour, in the eyes of senior university faculty.

The pranks, that included a flooded bathroom and a poodle dyed red, did threaten to get out of hand. When we nearly knocked over the warden of the men's residence, giving a push start to my friend's Skoda, I was in serious trouble. I could have been expelled, but was reprieved, most likely as a result of the intervention of my brother-in-law Malcolm, an individual of high standing in the educational world and a renowned headmaster (also, a liberal who managed to circumvent the apartheid laws to include several black pupils at his school). While I was barred from university residence, I was permitted to complete my studies. Justine, my elder sister, and her husband Malcolm were a positive influence on me: highly respected liberals who worked within the system. Their daughter Amanda Armstrong became a prominent lawyer, and was commis-sioned by Nelson Mandela to help draft the democratic constitution after the apartheid system ended in the 1990s.

Once graduated, I realized that South Africa under the apartheid regime was not the place for me. I hatched a plan to sell everything I owned, work in London for a while to save money, then move to Canada and become a lumberjack. London in the 1960s, however, had more attractions than I expected. There was Beatlemania, hippy love and young women in miniskirts. Being a rock'n'roll fan with anti-authoritarian tendencies didn't get me into trouble, it got me in with the cool set. It was a kind of heaven. At the time, I bene-fited from what nowadays is referred to as white privilege; that is to say, as a young white man with a degree, a native English speaker, it was easy in London to find employment.

I gravitated to a region of west London around the Bayswater Road, dubbed Kangaroo Valley, as it was where many young Australians rented rooms and socialized as part of a tour of Europe. I discovered that a favoured, low-cost way of touring the conti-nent was to convert a secondhand van into a camper, and take to the roads with a group of friends. This struck me as a tremendous idea. From my wages I saved some money, bought an old grocery delivery van, and with the help of a scrap merchant and some ingenuity, converted it into a basic camper van. I put up advertisements in the embassies of Australia and South Africa, inviting fellow travellers.

There were four of us, all South African: two friends, Hazel and Alison, and Glen, Alison's cousin. I dubbed it the Dongervogel – a concocted Afrikaans word approximately translating to 'the bird of the ditches" (I cannot recall why). We set off: around England, Wales and Scotland, then across in the ferry to Scandinavia. Hazel and Alison slept in a tent while Glen and I slept on the roof rack in fine weather, or in the van when it rained. Norway and Sweden were very expensive for visitors from the UK, and learning to be economical was a valuable learning experience.

After the tour of Europe, two significant things happened: I secured a 'proper' job, with a salary and prospects; and I realized that I did not wish to live without Hazel, one of the travel companions. She felt the same way, and the two of us were married on 1 January 1970 in Hampstead Registry Office, the most perfect day and occasion for me. Two years later our first child was born. Two more children were to follow. Within a quite short space of time, I had undergone a conversion from bohemian wishing to see the world and chop down trees in the wilds of British Columbia, to a suburban commuter with a young family, indistinguishable from the thousands of other university-educated young men with similar corporate roles. But deep down, I still considered myself African.

My earliest full-time professional role was in sales at the petrochemical giant Esso, which took us to the west of England and to Wales, before relocating us back in London. The most significant learning experience from this period of my career came from observing a model approach to negotiation by a more senior manager. This took place at the large petrochemical refinery at Milford Haven on the west coast of Wales. It was a unionized workplace and the manager in question had to deal with noises of potential industrial action in response to a pay offer that he regarded has fair, and the most that could be reasonably afforded. He was neither confrontational nor submissive; he did not attempt to manipulate or sow division, but calmly made a case and asked that the proposal be put to the workers. He explained to others on the management side that the first offer was also the fall-back – an unconventional approach at the time. He took the trouble to address the workers as adults, explaining the commercial and market situation and supporting his case with documentation. The majority could see it was a good offer and the threat of strikes passed. This is a timeless lesson to me in negotiation: be calm, be factual, be fair, don't play games. The approach may not always be sufficient, but it gives you the best chance of avoiding either confrontation or political complexity when dealing with others.

In 1985 my father, who had been enjoying his travels in warm locations during his retirement – he always disliked the cold of the European winter – became very ill. He returned to the UK, was diagnosed with terminal cancer and died in a nursing home shortly afterwards. He was philosophical about his fate and spent his last days in a care home with some dignity.

My father's passing seemed to propel me towards a new phase of my life, and I began to look for new opportunities, having been with Esso for 17 years. I applied for a job at the European HQ of the Diagnostics Division (ADD) of Abbott Laboratories in Wiesbaden, near Frankfurt, to take on a leadership development role in the marketing department. Hazel was keen to live in a new country. My children initially found the relocation difficult but quickly learned German, made friends and flourished. Subsequently we moved to the USA when I took up a new role at Abbott's HQ in Chicago, running a corporate training program. We moved in 1989.

One of the most rewarding and significant spells at Abbott, in the light of subsequent developments in my career, was in the period spent implementing total quality in the 1990s. The managerial approach of 'total quality management' originated in the 1950s among post-war US advisers in Japan, and became fashionable across the western business world in the 1980s, following the international success of many Japanese manufacturers. It has its detractors and supporters. My experience is that the difference in its effectiveness lies more in the delivery than in the concept. As with all approaches to management, each intervention is different. Total quality is often associated with a tightly organized approach to manufacturing production lines, insisting on zero defects. A broader approach is to adopt the discipline of seeing the world from the customer's point of view, and working back from that to ensure that they receive the highest quality and most appropriate service. It is an approach that values empathy as well as precision, qualitative insights as well as quantitative data.

A valuable principle is never to assume what the customer wants, and instead take the trouble to find out. At Abbott, we advised the diagnostics division on total quality. They were supplying test equipment to medical laboratories to help diagnose a range of conditions, such as diabetes and AIDS. We were responsible for maintenance. We initially employed an apparently rational quality target of minimizing response times when equipment needed repair. The approach was backed by data, and we decided to test its effectiveness by matching it against customers' needs and preferences. This produced a surprise: we discovered that as response times became shorter, customer satisfaction ratings went down. The quicker we were getting technicians to the laboratories to fix a registered problem, the more annoyed our customers were becoming. What was going on?

We engaged in conversations, including hosting focus groups with representatives of our customers, viewed through a one-way mirror. What transpired is that response time was not a helpful indicator. These were important tests, often being carried out on critically ill patients. The laboratories had backup – they had to because the patients often had serious conditions and were vulnerable, so if there was a fault with a machine they had to switch immediately to another. If technicians arrived during a procedure, they were a nuisance; it was more helpful for them to arrive when there was downtime. The critical issue was not the response time, but the timing of the response.

Extraordinarily, senior management had expressed skepticism over introducing total quality on account of its cost. Once this customer-sensitive approach to helping the laboratories had been adopted, we were able to demonstrate that costs actually came down, because we were no longer paying highly skilled technicians to be kept in a waiting room. Moreover, service improved. The approach saved us millions, and it made the customers very happy.

Management processes then – and almost certainly still, in many cases – can be affected by a tendency to improve efficiency and automation in thoughtless ways, which can mean doing the wrong things more quickly. It is always necessary to ensure that data reflects reality, and that what you are measuring helps improve service. It is remarkable how often organizations, large and small, in all sectors, are prone to experiencing sustained lapses in these basic disciplines.

I have always been of the view that no genuine learning goes wasted. Some aspects of organizational and human behaviour are timeless, and applicable in any context and culture. The insights that I gleaned working with the test laboratories – on the importance of understanding the real customer needs and configuring operations around these requirements, and of balancing data with qualitative insights – were to help Africa Bridge projects survive and flourish on several occasions many years later.

Towards the end of my tenure at Abbott, the work was less rewarding. I was promoted to a role as director of learning, but the requirements of this heavily regulated sector meant I was progressively occupied with the need to stay up-to-date with compliance. During this period, while my sense of satisfaction at work dipped, I became more engaged with seminars and meetings organized by the Synchronicity movement, after reading the book *Synchronicity: The Inner Path of Leadership* by Joe Jaworski. Synchronicity is a philosophy of transformational leadership that is based on the understanding that we, as conscious human agents and as leaders, have the capacity not merely to anticipate and react to the future, but to imagine and create a better one. This is a concept in line with the Nelson Mandela quote cited earlier in the chapter: poverty is not inevitable; it can be ended with sufficient collective will.

Becoming part of the Synchronicity movement was to have a life-changing impact, because it was during the process of attending these seminars and meetings, both as delegate and on occasion as speaker, that the idea of Africa Bridge began to take shape. It was through the Synchronicity meetings that I met Reola Phelps, who advised me at Abbott and became a friend of Hazel and myself, and who later joined Africa Bridge, where she continues to work for us some two decades later. In another significant event, at a public leadership seminar in Chicago, a group of African-American delegates approached me and said: 'We like it when you talk about Africa.' I was astounded because I could not recall doing so. It must have been an aside during a longer talk.

In my journal from around this time one entry reads:

Go to Africa

My calling is Africa

Go..... deal with the excuses later

I must find the courage to cross the threshold

I reflected that I had not visited Tanzania since leaving in 1962. I discussed the matter with Hazel, and she felt similarly that she wanted to 'do something' – we shared a vague but powerful ambition.

It was time to go home.

CHAPTER 12
EARLY YEARS – 2
SETTING UP AFRICA BRIDGE

A ttending the same public leadership conference as the African-American delegates who asked me to talk more about Africa, was a young woman who had just returned from Tanzania. She had been working for a missionary doctor, Dr Mark Jacobson, at the Selian Lutheran Hospital, located near Arusha, the city where I had attended school as a boy. She asked me to contact Mark and offer to help the Selian to acquire much-needed medical equipment. I emailed Mark and asked him what help he needed. We decided that it would make sense for me to try and acquire hospital laboratory equipment. I was able to do this through my contacts in the Diagnostics division. Together with another wonderful man, Dr Rick Schiefelbein, who was the pathologist at the Port Angeles Hospital in Washington State, we equipped and trained Selian Lab and lab technicians with some essential diagnostic instrumentation. The Selian had been a dispensary, founded in the 1950s. In 1985 Mark joined the clinic and began to transform the facility into what became a 120-bed full-service hospital.

In September 1998 Mark asked me, 'When was the last time you were in Tanzania?' I responded: '1962.' He said that I needed to return to my homeland. My response was: what did he want me to do? Did he and his staff want leadership training, or Total Quality Management, or something else? He said, 'We need nothing more from you Barry. You have forgotten how to be an African. Just come back.'

In December 1998 I made my first visit to Tanzania since leaving school three and a half decades earlier. Dr Mark Jacobson and his wife Linda made me welcome at their home in Arusha, and I met many other individuals, including Jackson, the Laboratory Manager, and Mao, who was my driver and guide for much of the visit. I learned of an education program for Masai children, with particular focus on girls, prompting thoughts about leadership development. I visited my former school in Arusha; I saw the trees I used to climb, and the dormitory in which I had slept. Sadly the building itself was in a state of physical disrepair, although the teacher who conducted my tour, Anthony Mamiro, was an inspirational individual. I was able to include a visit to Tanga, where I visited some friends of Mark and Linda, and was able to see my former family home by the harbour. The garden was a little less tidy, but the bougainvillea plants were still flourishing.

In the conversations I held during my trip in December 1998, I learned of many initiatives to do with health and education, met many wonderful people, and had many conversations on the potential for Tanzania. There was infinite potential, and seemingly infinite options. There were also obstacles: I heard about corruption and bureaucracy; the lack of basic elements of infrastructure for much of the population, including water and electricity; the humanitarian tragedy that was AIDS, and the low life expectancy for many Tanzanians. On the road back from Tanga to Arusha, a policeman stopped our vehicle and asked for a ride, as he needed to transport prisoners some 25 km down the road. A while later, another policeman asked us for the same favour. Both were polite and we had no issue helping them, but this was another sobering illustration of the lack of resources for public services.

At some point I would have to focus, be selective, and choose an initiative. But in my mind and heart there was a growing conviction that 'I have to do something'. My journal from the time also outlined some potential ideas for what this 'something' might consist of:

- A scenario planning session for Tanzania's future.
- A Synchronicity-style conference in Dar es Salaam, representing all sectors of the economy.
- A grass-roots leadership program involving activities in Tanzania and overseas experience for the nation's leaders.
- An initiative involving Mark, Mao and Jackson at the Selian Hospital.
- Further research in the village communities, learning about grass-roots issues.
- Helping doctors run hospitals through leadership development programs.

The journal records that I reflected on the three principles of Bill O'Brien, an inspirational speaker I had heard at a Synchronicity event: 1) drive out greed, 2) know yourself and stay connected, and 3) serve out of yourself.

Back in the USA, the sense of purpose and fulfilment in my senior corporate training role continued to diminish, serving to underline an impending change of direction. In the spring of 2000, Hazel and I attended a private retreat hosted by Sheryl Erickson, whom we knew through the Synchronicity movement, at a terrific venue by the sea in New England, attended by other followers of the movement. We talked about how the West and Africa could learn from each other. This prompted the metaphor of a bridge. It is a connection with two-way traffic, a pleasing symbol of equity and interchange. As the discussion continued – there was a group of around 10 of us – we became more impassioned about the idea. The other individuals formed a physical bridge with their raised arms through which Hazel and I danced. This spontaneous ritual confirmed our commitment and our ambition. Another individual at the retreat was Dorothy Keville, an influential HIV/AIDS activist based in Washington DC, who volunteered to help the fledgling Africa Bridge. Also in spring 2000, at an Abbott management conference, I received an invitation to a talk in Toronto to be given by Archbishop Desmond Tutu, the veteran anti-apartheid campaigner of whom I was a longstanding admirer. Abbott gave me two tickets, and Dorothy Keville also attended. We secured a short meeting with the archbishop – a truly memorable moment. I told him of my ambitions to help social and economic development in Africa and in subsequent correspondence he wrote expressing his support and approval – which gave us a tremendous lift.

Just over a month later, at the end of June 2000, I took a retirement package from Abbott – although still only in my 50s – and set up the inaugural board of Africa Bridge. This consisted of myself, Hazel, Reola Phelps, Dorothy Keville, Mark Jacobson and Curt Kirkemo, a director of research at Abbott Laboratories. Six months later we had secured charitable status. It was exhilarating. It was also daunting and at times I felt vulnerable. I had autonomy but no organization. As I began preparatory work, I had some problems with my computer: there was no IT department to contact!

An early decision was to see Africa Bridge as a journey of discovery, rather than a specific project, and not to commit rigidly to a single plan. There were several missteps in the early years, but this was one of the good decisions. It kept us continually learning and adapting. The first, and most pressing need was to gather more intelligence. In late 2000 I returned to Africa to engage in a series of exploratory meetings and interviews, visiting both South Africa and Tanzania.

In total, I carried out 30 formal and 25 informal interviews. One of the most helpful meetings was in Cape Town with Dr Daniel

Nycynyama, at that time editor of the principal South African medical journal. He described how Western initiatives sometimes struggle in Africa by adopting assumptions of Western methods and infrastructure. He said to me:

'You know Barry, we in South Africa have had all the resources donated to us that we need to solve the HIV/AIDS problem in South Africa. However, there are two problems. First, all the resources that come here have a Western agenda. How they are to be spent is decided in London, Paris or Washington DC. That agenda might make sense in the West, but it does not necessarily make sense here. Second, we as South Africans have not decided what we want to do about HIV/AIDS.'

Another interview shed light on why some people were not seeking to be tested for HIV. I was told:

'If I live in a slum, in a cardboard shanty, my neighbor may accidentally knock over his candle tonight. The fire will spread rapidly to my cardboard hut and kill me. In the morning I get up and go to the corner of the block to catch the taxi to work. I could be stabbed to death. The taxi is an overloaded dilapidated minibus in which I have a good chance of dying. If I am lucky, I will save enough money to go home for Christmas. The bus I will travel in is a death trap. So what is this thing called AIDS that may kill me in five to 14 years' time? Furthermore, if I contract HIV/AIDS, why should I get tested? If I am positive, I will be cast out by society, I will lose my job. What good is the test?'

I recorded at the time that those in denial of the spread of HIV infection, and its impact on individuals and families, were not just the people living in the shanty towns. The attitude was also prevalent among well-educated men and women in positions of influence. Some of the strongest denial was among white people. In many regions of the continent, there was not the infrastructure in place to support a Western-style approach – such as a network of well-resourced hospitals and clinics in every town. Many villages and towns needed to build up their local economy so that they could fund or develop ingenious alternatives to the top-down distribution and dissemination that might work in a Western nation. An early idea I had was to arrange a symposium for leaders of different sectors, from Tanzanian institutions and representatives of international organizations. Fortunately, no one wanted to fund it – I judge now that such a 'top-down' initiative would have gotten Africa Bridge off to a poor start. Another potential project, more in tune with local practices, was the idea for wider use of herbal medicines to curb symptoms of AIDS, after learning that a highly effective treatment developed by specialist Bongo Mzizi had been approved by the World Health Organization. As discussed in Chapter 9 Continual Learning, this did not take off, despite Bongo's clinic being established within a hospital and receiving referrals from doctors.

It was clear that there was much learning to do, and that an essential quality for us all on the board of Africa Bridge was humility.

These early meetings did confirm some founding principles. One was the concept of being adaptable, rather than fixated on a certain project; the other was the idea of ensuring equal representation of women in Africa Bridge initiatives. In matters of sex, most women in Africa had little choice, for example on whether men wore condoms. HIV / AIDS was taking a bigger toll on women than men. I noted at the time that we had to ensure that in all activities women had an equal stake. The problems were so great they would require the thinking, perspectives and skills of both genders in equal proportions.

In these early months, we settled on three principles:

a) Integrate intellect, emotions and spirit.

b) Include all sectors.

c) Act local but think global.

Back in the USA, Hazel and I had the wonderful opportunity to meet Margaret Wheatley, an inspirational teacher on leadership, at her home in Utah. It was at this meeting that we learned of the potential of Future Search as the basis for establishing a project. It is based on universal principles of human engagement, so does not depend on a certain culture or level of infrastructure. If anything, in villages in Tanzania with strong levels of community cohesion, it may be particularly effective. The cornerstone principles are: to analyse the problems locally, nationally and globally; to define and understand the reality; to identify the future you wish to create; and to discuss how to move from the present reality to the future state (see Chapter 3 How Africa Bridge Operates for a description of how Future Search is used in Africa Bridge projects).

In September 2001 I returned to Africa, this time accompanied by Hazel. It was more vacation than work, as we were attending a family gathering to mark my eldest sister Justine's 70th birthday. In addition we took some trips to see wildlife. Unfortunately, it was marred by Hazel contracting African sleeping sickness following a bite from a tsetse fly while on safari at the Tarangire Game Park in Tanzania. There were rushes to hospital, and many hours of pain and discomfort for her and anxiety for us all. The treatment is not a complete cure but she did respond well and made a recovery. We were such a close couple, having been together for 30 years, that this was a major shock.

Ironically, it was upon our return to the States that Africa Bridge was to make a significant step forward. I received an email from a young Tanzanian woman, Neema Mgana, who was studying for a Master's in public health at Loma Linda University near Los Angeles. She had heard about the Africa Bridge initiative and recommended that I visit Idweli, a Tanzanian village affected by a high rate of orphans, to conduct a needs assessment and co-operate with a small charity called Godfrey's Children Organization, named after a young doctor who had died tragically young. We arranged some meetings in the US, between Hazel, me, Neema and some of her friends, beginning a most promising partnership. Also during this period, I attended a Future Search facilitator training course in Philadelphia.

Towards the end of 2001, I returned to Tanzania and met Fred, Godfrey's brother, and Furaha, a good friend, who were both volunteers and board members for Godfrey's Children. They introduced me to Mr Ngeka, the Village Chairman. The initial Future Search meeting in Idweli is described in Chapter 3. In parallel with that process, it was necessary to establish a workable constituency of support – effectively an informal 'licence to operate' within the country. The track record of Europeans and North Americans offering aid and assistance in deprived parts of sub-Saharan Africa is uneven. As Dr Nycynyama had informed me, one problem is a Western design that is not always suitable. In one illustration of this, a couple of years later, after the orphanage had been set up in Idweli, I had the idea of engaging older adults as surrogate grandparents, volunteers to befriend the orphans. This was borrowed from a successful initiative in Chicago, where reciprocal bonds of friendship and support had been mutually beneficial. In Idweli, however, it failed to engage. This was because the orphans often had their real grandparents living nearby, and no elderly people wanted to move away from their homes. This is a good example of a Western idea being ineffective in a different culture, where there was more material poverty but stronger family and community bonds. I do not believe it did any harm, but learning that acts of compassion can be ineffective or even counter-productive is a difficult lesson. All those in the development and caring professions could make a pledge similar to that of the medical profession: 'First, do no harm.'

Another problem with some Western aid projects is lack of staying power – the mission is for a year or two, or five, or a planned long-term project is folded. We wanted to make a lasting, permanent difference, but to convince people to work with you, you have to establish trust. Some of the irregularities that we were to experience in the early months of the first projects – bricks being stolen from a building project, money going missing with the carrier reporting to have been mugged – were frustrating, but understandable in a situation where Europeans with their aid projects are often not around for long, and people have learned to be opportunistic. If trust is to be built, it has to work both ways. We worked to establish relationships of trust with local politicians and officials – for example, in Idweli, Mr Ngeka the Village Chairman, Felix the Village Executive Officer, and Alice the Ward Community Development Officer. The relationships Hazel and I established with Neema, and the introductions that she made, were part of this process. A crucial development a couple of years later was the appointment of Martha Mmbando, recommended to me by Joel Strauss, a former Peace Corps volunteer in the 1960s and a long-standing aid worker for USAID. Martha became our first employee in 2003, working as a highly effective facilitator and interpreter. She worked with Africa Bridge until 2018. Such well qualified and long-serving staff represent a priceless asset for any organization, and especially for aid and development projects.

During the visit in late 2001, I returned to Arusha to meet my friends Mark and Linda Jacobson. We visited the Selian Hospital again, and accompanied Paulina, the hospice nurse, both at the Selian and on her rounds within the community. She was an impressively dedicated and caring individual. It was a sobering, at times shocking visit. Around 80% of cases were HIV/AIDS, a dramatic increase compared with three years earlier. There was no funding for antiretroviral drugs. Some individuals were in a desperate state. We met Bariki, the AIDS patient who was dying (see Chapter 1), due to leave two children in the care of a frail grandmother. We also met a young carer, just nine years old, whose mother, not an AIDS patient, was paralyzed in both legs, one arm and her face. The girl looked after her sick family with impressive dedication and intelligence, and was dreaming of gaining an education and becoming a teacher.

It was becoming clearer to me that the mission of Africa Bridge was about transforming the wellbeing of vulnerable children in Tanzania. This made sense to me, deep down at a visceral level. This was the land that had formed and nurtured me. I had been blessed by a wonderful childhood in Tanzania. My children were all grown up and charting their own way in life. My mission was to give back to the people and to the land that had been so generous to me as a child.

CONCLUSION
A MODEL FOR SOCIAL POLICY AND ECONOMIC DEVELOPMENT

Independent researchers indicate that Africa Bridge has some features that it shares with other projects; however they also find that its particular combination is probably unique. This conclusion resulted from a literature review by MarketShare Associates, assessed in combination with the researchers' own knowledge and work with similar enterprises. Other enterprises have involved identifying vulnerable households and helping with the provision of an asset or interest-free loan and coaching and training, to create a 'pathway out of poverty' towards economic self-reliance. There are numerous agricultural co-operative initiatives in many countries, established in rural areas for the benefit of those on low incomes. Also, there are many initiatives targeted at helping most vulnerable children, especially to gain education. The two features that appear to be unique to Africa Bridge are the requirement to pass on an asset, and the close links and co-operation between the agricultural co-operatives and the Most Vulnerable Children's Committees.[1]

The MarketShare Associates' report identifies key tactics that are used. Addressed at the level of principles, some of the key elements that are features of Africa Bridge, and that the research shows are effective, are:

- Building on inherent strengths; recognizing the potential within.
- Resilience and learning from experience.
- Deploying the strengths and expertise of Barry and Africa Bridge founders.
- Combining business and social goals.
- Making improved prospects for children the central goal.
- Passion and a sense of purpose.
- Being patient – showing that you are committed to the long term.

The Africa Bridge approach has distinctive characteristics that mark it out, not only from many other approaches at combatting poverty, but from traditional social policies also. By making the most vulnerable children the focus, and creating improved opportunities for them the strategic priority, this inverts many traditional approaches which focus on land, resources, technology and job opportunities for adults, with children and communities expected to fit around them.

There is growing recognition, supported by findings from Africa Bridge and elsewhere, that the most sustainable, effective, and equitable approaches to economic development are geared around enhanced prospects and quality of life, rather than traditional economic indicators such as income growth and GDP. Also, findings show that it is more useful to track impact by project, rather than by region or nation. As well as being a game-changer for Africa, this approach may contain valuable lessons and insights for policymakers more widely.

We encourage others to copy, or be inspired by, our projects. The Africa Bridge model is not protected by copyright – we welcome imitators! We also welcome innovations and ideas for improvement. We hope that by being open in sharing our operational details and research findings in this book, there will be many such initiatives, and that others will benefit from the lessons learned, not only in

Tanzania and east Africa, but wherever there is the need. It is unacceptable for a single child or household to suffer hunger or diminished prospects for a healthy and fulfilling life. Collectively, as human societies, we have the resources and the body of knowledge to end this scourge everywhere.

ABOUT THE AUTHORS

Barry Childs grew up in Tanzania, the son of a British agricultural adviser. After graduating from the University of Kwa Zulu Natal in Pietermaritzburg, South Africa, he moved to the UK. A successful career in corporate management, including spells at oil giant Exxon (UK) and healthcare company Abbott, took him to from the UK to Germany and the USA. His business experience was in multiple functions leading to a concentration in organizational development and total quality management. In 2000, he decided to take early retirement from corporate life and devote the latter part of his career to humanitarian projects to improve life prospects for those on lowest incomes in Tanzania, the country of his childhood. After several years of team building, research, piloting income generating activities and psychosocial interventions, he developed the Africa Bridge model to transform the lives of most vulnerable children.

Philip Whiteley is an experienced business author, in a career spanning more than 30 years, mostly in the field of leadership, organizational development and sustainability. He is an approved supplier for the International Institute for Management Development (IMD) based in Lausanne Switzerland. In 2022 he was the author of the landmark publication *Fifty for Fifty*, IMD's publication to mark the 50th anniversary of its MBA. The book *Deliver What You Promise* (Heligo 2022) by Bali Padda, former COO of LEGO, for which Philip was editorial consultant, was shortlisted for the Business Book of the Year award in the UK in 2023. He is a member of the Society of Authors.

ACKNOWLEDGMENTS

For a project that spans a quarter of a century there are hundreds of people who have been involved in the development and progression of Africa Bridge. Many of them I know. I am also conscious that there are many I do not know who have helped in the evolution of the model.

FAMILY

Thank you to my mother who taught me the meaning of unconditional love, and my father for giving me a sense of humor, and a love of nature and of Africa.

Thank you to Hazel, my late wife, who was a rock upon which Africa Bridge was formed, launched and developed. She empowered me to embark on this adventure, handle the adversities, maintain my efforts, and celebrate the victories.

Thank you, Kathy, who risked marrying this alien jungle boy and totally embraced the concept and functionality of Africa Bridge. Kathy generously supports Africa Bridge with her philanthropy and advocacy for the effectiveness and sustainability of the model in transforming the lives of vulnerable children.

Thank you to my children Ruth, Rowan and Robert, for their love and the lessons they have taught me, and to my sister Jennifer, who has stood by her baby brother and the windmills he has tilted at.

TANZANIANS

Thank you to all the Tanzanian children. You are the most important people we encounter. You are the future of your communities and country. Your joy, laughter and transparency are an inspiration to us all.

Thank you, parents and host families of the vulnerable children. Thank you to the over 300 volunteer Most Vulnerable Children's Committee members serving vulnerable children and their families in 37 villages, and to the Empowerment Facilitators acting as our representatives within the villages we serve.

Among the hundreds of Tanzanians who have supported me and Africa Bridge are Amon Mwalupindi, retired Ward Councilor of Isongole Ward, who is one of the most skillful individuals I have ever worked with in handling tough, potentially adversarial situations, and Mama Mende, past District Commissioner of Rungwe District, whose prompt and effective skills saved our Tanzanian staff and me from the threat of violence. Also thank you to our Tanzanian staff and board members.

Thank you to all Tanzanians for the love, compassion and consideration you have given me as a child and as a returning elder. The name Africa Bridge implies that what we are doing is focused on the land where my character was formed, and that the traffic on a bridge is two-way. Westerners have resources and processes to give, and Tanzanians inform us about humility, compassion and respect for others.

PARTNERS

Throughout this journey, the local Tanzanian government has been our ongoing partner: from early attempted projects in the Tanga Region, to our 20-year history with the Rungwe and Busokelo Districts of Mbeya Region. We have worked closely with village, ward, and district officials representing administration, social services, agriculture, education, health, and community development. Much of the success of the model stems from this productive partnership.

Other partners include: the Lundy Foundation, which joined with us in the creation of Idweli Godfrey's Children Center; the Rungwe Lutheran and Moravian churches, which assisted us in piloting the early co-ops; and the Human Development Trust, which assisted in the establishment of the first most Vulnerable Children's Committees. Veterinarians without Borders helped establish a timely supply chain for vaccines to prevent the spread of animal diseases.

DONORS

This group includes family, friends and individuals who have found us as we developed the model. Foundations and associations that have been regular supporters include the Abbott Fund, the Miller Family Foundation, Newman's Own Foundation, Rotary International, the Rotary Club of Lake Oswego and many other Rotary clubs worldwide, the Segal Family Foundation, and Vibrant Village.

FRIENDS, VOLUNTEERS, BOARD MEMBERS, STAFF AND ASSOCIATES

Africa Bridge has become a big part of who I am and my friends have rallied to expedite this journey. The friends include: Curt Kirkemo, who helped navigate organizational issues; Dr Mark Jacobson who reminded me that I am an African by nature; and John O'Lear, whom I thank for his wise counsel.

Thank you to all our volunteers, board members, staff, and associates for all the hours, imagination and care you have dedicated to this organization.

Thank you to Mark Morford at Stoel Rives and Chris Rich of

Perkins Coie for your voluntary leadership and legal guidance; to Ellen Worcester and Susan Stewart for reeling the ideas in and helping make sense of them; to Sharon Brabenac, who became Executive Director during a major crisis, dug her feet in, and started figuring out how to raise the phoenix from the ashes. Thanks also to Reola Phelps, who has helped to facilitate a passage through complex situations arising from that crisis. She has steadied the ship, creating the conditions for a new course. Thank you to Carl Sardegna and Pat Castleman for applying their business experiences to finding a fresh approach to fund raising.

Thank you to all the sub-contractors, academic institutions and researchers who have contributed to the development of the model.

Thanks to all those angels who have helped us to find a path through what seemed to be impossible barriers. A consistent mystery is that there is no knowing who you may turn out to be and how you know when to make your interventions.

Thank you to my co-author Philip Whiteley, who has helped me to articulate how the unconscious knowledge gained as a child and young adult in Africa, intermingled with the conscious business experiences gained in two large international corporations, combined to generate the Africa Bridge model. A blend of the soft and the hard.

Thank you, all the children, angels, family, friends, volunteers, board members, staff, donors, associates and partners. Thank you all from the bottom of my heart and God bless you all.

Barry Childs

WHAT THEY SAY ABOUT
AFRICA BRIDGE

Archbishop Desmond Tutu, writing in 2005
'I was moved when Barry Childs spoke to me some years ago of his dream to help children orphaned by HIV/AIDS and their families in Tanzania. By helping the most disadvantaged, Africa Bridge performs much needed divine work, letting the poorest of the poor know they are loved. There is no higher calling.'

Archbishop Desmond Tutu, 1931-2021, humanitarian church leader and anti-apartheid campaigner. Awarded the Nobel Peace Prize in 1984.

Dr Heath Prince

'Africa Bridge does what precious few other programs have managed to do – it lifts children out of poverty, allowing them to tap into their full potential, and setting them on a course to break the intergenerational cycles of poverty that have robbed them and their communities of the opportunity to live lives of their own choosing, rather than those determined by privation. Founded on love, ingenuity, and dedication, Africa Bridge's impressive success gives the lie to the lazy assertions that the problem of poverty is unsolvable.'

Dr Heath Prince, PhD Director, Ray Marshall Center, University of Texas at Austin, and Senior Development Economist at La Isla Network.

Lwitiko Kadenge Mwalukumba

'In 2008 I dreamed of becoming a doctor. However, I had struggled to even go to primary school. I could not imagine how I would be able to attend high school and university. I felt I was trapped. With the arrival of Africa Bridge in my village of Igembe, my dream became a reality.'

Dr Lwitiko Kadenge Mwalukumba, Igembe Village.

Tunsi Belega

'The women in our corn co-op began to realize that we were growing higher yielding corn than the men. We concluded if we could grow better corn than the men, we could do anything better than them.'

Tunsi Belega, Africa Bridge farmer and entrepreneur, Lufumbi Village.

Jacob and Garannetti Mwakakipesile

'Our cow called Hope gave us the resources we need to ensure all our six grandchildren receive a high school education and have the opportunity to go to university.'

Jacob and Garannetti Mwakakipesile, Bujesi Village.

Granny Witness

'Look what the pig did – she has made it possible for me to build a new concrete brick house with a tin roof and real furniture. She also helped me to build three shops which I can rent, which gives me regular income.'

Granny Witness, Idweli Village.

AND THE CHILDREN SHALL LEAD US 149

. . .

Femida Kupda

'The [Africa Bridge] program really benefited our community. We faced a challenge of absenteeism, where many children were unable to attend school sessions due to a lack of school supplies; but since Africa Bridge supported us with the supplies, children now attend school regularly.'

Femida Kupda, Empowerment Facilitator, Mbambo Village, Kambasegela Ward.

Theresia Mgimbo, Headteacher

'With Africa Bridge's help in the villages, people have income from selling milk and they can now support children with school needs.'

Theresia Mgimbo Kisondela Secondary School Head Mistress.

Susan Newman

'Africa Bridge is the embodiment of an organization's successful blueprint to address the harsh realities of under-served families and children in Tanzania. They provide the capital and training to deliver self-empowerment, self-sufficiency and sustainability.'

Susan Kendall Newman, Newman's Own Foundation Community Partners' Program Participant.

Julitha Mupwa

'The Africa Bridge projects have helped our community to change their perspective on the stereotype that a woman is not able to keep a dairy cow. Now the community believes that a woman can manage to keep any kind of cattle.'

Julitha Mupwa, Kambasegela Village.

. . .

Kisa Stambule Kajuni

'Thank you to Africa Bridge for giving us support to include knowledge on parenting, and for the modern ways of project shed construction and care for chickens.'

Kisa Stambule Kajuni, Isuba Village, Kisondela.

Ben Fowler

'We had the opportunity to study the Africa Bridge model through an endline evaluation we conducted of one of its latest initiatives. Having lived in and worked on a variety of initiatives providing support in rural East Africa, what I find particularly noteworthy about the Africa Bridge model is the commitment to a time-bound period of support and careful selection of communities with strong need, but also commitment to change. By not planning to stay in a community indefinitely, Africa Bridge remains focused on identifying the most effective inputs that will help to kickstart an ongoing and community-led development process.'

Ben Fowler, Co-Founder and CEO, MarketShare Associates.

Carl Sardegna

'Barry Childs has successfully integrated business strategies with his first-hand knowledge of the Tanzanian culture to create a proven process that is a game changer in the struggle to create a cost-effective model to alleviate extreme poverty in sub-Saharan Africa.'

Carl Sardegna, retired CEO Blue Cross Blue Shield, Maryland, and retired CEO Green Crescent Insurance.

Gary Grossman

'Africa Bridge charts a transformative course in rural community

AND THE CHILDREN SHALL LEAD US   151

development, one that balances the scales between economic sustainability and social welfare. Rooted in the belief of a hand up and not a handout, Africa Bridge enriches entire communities, starting with empowering their most vulnerable members. From the 'pass-on' concept through agricultural co-ops to the deeply engaged Most Vulnerable Children's Committees, the organization's innovative strategies ensure that its impact resonates through generations. The book eloquently captures this unique, holistic, and ground-up approach, leaving the reader inspired and informed. A must-read for anyone interested in an effective, long-lasting model of positive change.'

Gary Grossman, Public Relations and Marketing Executive.

Peter Collett

'Barry and I were both born in Africa – him in Tanzania, me in Zambia. We attended the same boarding school and university in South Africa, and we've been in close contact ever since. Growing up in a colonial environment, we were constantly being told by those who thought they knew better that modern, advanced societies were the sole source of innovation, and that if you wanted to identify new approaches to old problems, you'd be advised to look for them in countries like Britain, Germany and the United States. Barry's book provides a fitting rebuttal to this preposterous idea, because it demonstrates – as the ancient Romans knew all too well – that there is always something new coming out of Africa. Not being content to follow in the footsteps of other aid practitioners, Barry has devised a totally novel, Africa-based business model – one that places local participants at the very heart of the process, empowering them by making them active partners, giving them dignity and responsibility, and enabling them to become, if not the authors, at least the co-authors of their own destiny.

'This timely book tells a truly fascinating story – how, with no seafaring experience to speak of, Barry managed to build the good ship Africa Bridge, so that he could help to alleviate the suffering of people in his native Tanzania. Tanzanians have a Swahili saying: *"asisafirie nyota ya mwenzio"*, which translates as, "don't set sail using someone else's star". That's exactly what Barry has done – he's found his own lodestar, and he's used it to guide the good ship Africa Bridge through the high seas and choppy waters of charity aid. May God continue to bless her, and all those who sail in her!'

Dr Peter Collett, Former Oxford Don, psychologist, author and broadcaster.

Dr Kenneth Lema

'I got to know Barry Childs in 2002 when colleagues from Abbott Laboratories introduced us. At that time, Barry had just retired from Abbott and he was keen to return and contribute to Tanzania's development, having grown up in the country when his father worked as an agricultural officer here in the 1940s and '50s. It was most interesting to hear his childhood experiences and memories and contrast them with today's Tanzania. Even more interesting were his opinions on African development challenges. For example, he believed the traditional advisory role of African elders was being progressively marginalized as African countries modernized. Given the weak societal institutions and reliance on oral history, this trend implied the loss of a key asset to African development. He was also a firm believer in participatory approaches to finding lasting solutions to issues facing African communities, rather than attempting to solve such issues using strategies and techniques that are alien to those communities. Driven by his love for Africa, and Tanzania in particular, Barry was keen to come back to Africa and contribute by identifying some key challenges in society, find the required resources in the developed world, then apply his own skills and theories, and so in a practical way demonstrate the effectiveness of such an approach. He had already set up Africa Bridge, a US-registered not-for-profit to implement his vision. I was immediately impressed by Barry's down-to-earth, practical and hands-on approach, and more so by his commitment to Tanzania, even after being away for so long. Therefore, I was keen to meet him and talk whenever he was in town, despite my busy work schedule. We have thus continued to be in touch by email and physically for the past 20 years and it has been a gratifying experience to see him translate the vision into reality through projects implemented by Africa Bridge.

'Back in 2002, Africa Bridge obtained a small grant from Abbott Fund that Barry used to start the initial project to support orphans and other vulnerable children (OVC) in Mbeya, Southwestern Tanzania. Working with relatively small grants, I have witnessed Africa Bridge establish one of the most successful programs for vulnerable children in the country. In this program a whole village participates in setting up what are called "Village OVC Committees" that are in effect the custodians of the vulnerable children's issues at the village level. [Through the Africa Bridge approach,] families that had almost no income have been transformed into relatively vibrant families, able to afford basic needs like school uniforms, medication, food etc. There are several examples of co-op members who were in dire financial circumstances before the co-ops, but who now enjoy the relative comfort of owning their own house, or a shop or a milling machine, can produce sufficient food, and are able to support children under their care to go to school, and otherwise meet their basic needs.

'It can be said that the Africa Bridge project in Tanzania has employed the right strategy to show one way to deal with the challenge of caring for an increasing number of OVCs in Africa in a cost effective and sustainable manner. However, all this would not have been possible without the vision, commitment, and hard work of Barry Childs. Barry is one of very few Americans I know who take the regular bus from Dar es Salaam to Mbeya (a 900km road trip).

His energy and enthusiasm is boundless. This has been extremely helpful in attracting others to emulate him, as result of which Africa Bridge's work is admired not only in Tanzania and in the US, but also in many other parts of the world. Personally, I have been hugely inspired by Barry and have benefited from his counsel in my professional work over the years.'

Dr Kenneth Lema, Retired NGO Executive and Founder Mpingo Lodge Selous.

NOTES

4. AFRICA BRIDGE EFFECTIVENESS

1. For example, see: Brand, Margie and Ben Fowler. *Pathways Out of Poverty: Using Value Chains to Move Vulnerable Households up the Economic Ladder.* January 28, 2011. Presentation at the 55th Installment of USAID's "Linking Small Firms to Competitiveness Strategies" Breakfast Seminar Series.

   Also: Fowler, Ben. *Pathways Out of Poverty: Tools for Value Chain Development Practitioners.* Washington: ACDI/VOCA and USAID, 2012. https://marketshare associates.com/tools-for-value-chain-development-practitioners.

6. CONTEXT

1. A comprehensive history of post-independence Tanzania is captured in the compendium *Development as Rebellion – A Biography of Julius Nyerere.*
2. Paget, Dan. Tanzania: Shrinking Space and Opposition Protest, *Journal of Democracy*: July 2017.
3. Arusha Declaration: https://en.wikipedia.org/wiki/Arusha_Declaration
4. Tanzania's Samia Suhulu Hassan gets Covid jab in policy reversal, BBC, 28 July 2021 https://www.bbc.co.uk/news/world-africa-57996155
5. Our World in Data https://ourworldindata.org/extreme-poverty
6. https://data.worldbank.org/indicator/SP.DYN.LE00.IN?locations=TZ
7. Statistics from Our World in Data https://ourworldindata.org/grapher/child-mortality-by-income-level-of-country?tab=chart&country=TZA
8. From Our World in Data https://ourworldindata.org/grapher/malnutrition-death-rates?tab=chart&country=TZA
9. The Turning Point in the AIDS Epidemic, Harvard School of Public Health 2013 https://www.hsph.harvard.edu/news/magazine/off-the-cuff-aids-kanki/
10. https://data.worldbank.org/indicator/SE.PRM.ENRR?locations=TZ
11. World Bank https://data.worldbank.org/indicator/SE.ADT.LITR.ZS?locations=TZ

7. THERE ARE NO SHORTCUTS

1. Malcolm Gladwell talk https://www.youtube.com/watch?v=1uB5PUpGzeY
2. Ericsson, A., and Charness, N., Expert Performance: Its Structure and Acquisition, *American Psychologist*, 49 (8) 725-747 https://psycnet.apa.org/doiLanding?doi=10.1037%2F0003-066X.49.8.725

3. Ericsson, A., The Influence of Experience and Deliberate Practice on the Development of Superior Expert Performance, Chapter 38 *The Cambridge Handbook of Expertise and Expert Performance*, CUP 2006 – available as pdf at: https://clinica.ispa.pt/ficheiros/areas_utilizador/user11/4_-_the_influence_of_experience_and_deliberate_practice_on_the_development_of_superior_expert_performance.pdf
4. Wikipedia contains a brief overview of the four stages of learning, with a list of academic references: https://en.wikipedia.org/wiki/Four_stages_of_competence
5. Daniel Pink, The Positive Power of Regret, The Times, 30 January 2022 https://www.thetimes.co.uk/article/the-positive-power-of-regret-how-thinking-negatively-can-actually-help-us-dqs0dx9w9

8. WOMEN: A LEADING ROLE

1. Sergent, K., Stajkovic, A. D., Women's leadership is associated with fewer deaths during the Covid-19 crisis: Quantitative and qualitative analysis of United States governors, *Journal of Applied Psychology*, Vol 105(8), August 2020, 771-783
2. Northouse, Peter G., *Leadership: Theory and Practice*, Ninth Edition, Sage Publications, February 2021
3. Hicks, D., Larson, C., Nelson, C., Olds, D., Johnston, E., The Influence of Collaboration on Program Outcomes: The Colorado Nurse-Family Partnership, *Evaluation Review*, 5 May 2008
4. Goleman, D., Boyatzis, R., Social Intelligence and the Biology of Leadership, *Harvard Business Review*, September 2008, https://hbr.org/2008/09/social-intelligence-and-the-biology-of-leadership
5. See for example Mathai, S., Mathai A. A., Neuroscience in HR: Steer and Take Charge, NHRD Network Journal, 27 November 2018, https://journals.sagepub.com/doi/abs/10.1177/2631454118802502

9. CONTINUAL LEARNING

1. Bridget Riley profile, BBC, 3 June 2021 https://www.bbc.co.uk/news/entertainment-arts-57332625?at_custom1=%5Bpost+type%5D&at_custom2=twitter&at_custom4=B7093730-C7AF-11EB-A97D-42B5BDCD475E&at_medium=custom7&at_custom3=%40BBCRadio4&at_campaign=64

10. LOVE IS A VERB

1. Cable, D., Helping Your Team Feel the Purpose in Their Work, *Harvard Business Review*, October 2019 https://hbr.org/2019/10/helping-your-team-feel-the-purpose-in-their-work

2. Hlupic, V., *The Management Shift*, Palgrave Macmillan 2014; and *Humane Capital*, Bloomsbury 2018. Numerous articles in academic and business titles. See for example https://www.hrmagazine.co.uk/content/features/humane-resources-interview-with-vlatka-hlupic

CONCLUSION

1. Transforming the Lives of the Most Vulnerable Children: A Summary of Findings from Africa Bridge's Kisondela Ward Endline Survey, Marketshare Associates 2021 See also earlier research by Marketshare https://marketshareassociates.com/tools-for-value-chain-development-practitioners/. More on the BRAC program in Bangladesh at: https://www.brac.net/program/wp-content/uploads/2021/09/UPG-programme-Bangladesh-overview.pdf

Printed in the USA
CPSIA information can be obtained
at www.ICGtesting.com
CBHW071803140324
5385CB00008B/130

9 781739 379377